♫ Ain't We Got Fun ♫

The Impact of Humankind's Flawed Evolution

H. Robert Dubman

ISBN: 1517402247
ISBN 13: 9781517402242
Library of Congress Control Number: 2015915486
CreateSpace Independent Publishing Platform
North Charleston, South Carolina

To my wife, Betty, who has always been my unwavering supporter and fan.

Contents

Preface

• • •

*What has been will be again, what has been done will be done again; there
is nothing new under the sun.*
　　　　　　　　　　　　—Ecclesiastes 1:9

There is nothing new in the world except the history that you do not know.
　　　　　　　　Harry S. Truman, *Mr. President* (1952)

Whether in medicine, economics, politics, climate issues, or international matters, the world has come to expect quick cures.
We demand quick cures! But quick cures, even when they appear
to be successful on the surface, are often short-lived and followed
by repeated cycles of the same recurring personal and societal ills.

Almost every social, political, or economic issue that surfaces nowadays has appeared time and time again and in various guises throughout history. Political leaders fail to examine history for what does and
does not work, in favor of the expediency of short-term results that will
mollify their constituents. It is all too easy and convenient to address

immediate and *urgent* symptoms and avoid the pain of longer—but permanent—cures.

> *Political events are shaped by history rather than vice versa.*
> *The Evolution of Everything*, Matt Ridley, evolutionary biologist.

My intent with this book is to present a brief narrative on the subject of each chapter to show how it reflects the drawbacks of humankind's limited evolution and the impact of those drawbacks on our world. Because what is written here is merely a primer on each subject, I encourage readers to conduct further research on their own.

Biblical references in this text are not meant to lend authority to the historical accuracy of any passage. Whether or not they stem from real events or not, the messages are universally relevant and timeless.

Finally, the subject matter of each chapter is not in any particular or sequential order. Each subject is treated individually as part of the premise of this book.

Above all, when reading each chapter, bear in mind that history is the only unbiased teacher that is above reproach. Human dilemmas, both individual and societal, derive from our collective failure to learn from history.

That men do not learn very much from the lessons of history is the most important of all the lessons of history.
—Aldous Huxley

The farther back you look, the farther forward you are likely to see.
—Winston Churchill

Introduction

. . .

Consequences, Good and Bad

Human life on earth is, if nothing else, a matter of priorities and ongoing choices. This is a plain observation that, on the surface, appears too simplistic to attract further attention.

The reality is that for every choice there are consequences that generally range somewhere between good and bad. If that were not the case, that is, if every alternative would be known to be either 100 percent good or 100 percent bad, there would be nothing to consider and no choices to make.

Purchasing a particular brand of coffee is generally contingent upon individual taste (the good alternative). The bad alternative may be a higher cost that is disregarded in favor of an individual's taste. This is a simplistic example that doesn't require much consideration, because only the individual purchaser is affected by the bad alternative, with no consequences to others.

However, there is more, a lot more, to be said on the subject of consequences. Each chapter in this book deals with choices that we make throughout life that ripple beyond any individual choice maker.

All too often, choices involve serious consequences, are driven by emotions and habit patterns, involve misdirected good intentions, and are made with superficial information that is oblivious to over-all impact. Such decisions, whether ultimately good or bad, are not made just by individuals but include corporations and governmental bureaucracies as well.

Chinese philosophy and medicine recognize seemingly opposite or contrary forces (yin and yang) that are found throughout nature, in-cluding within human conduct. Other religions and philosophies recognize similar contradictions and conundrums.

Today, in the early part of the twenty-first century, humanity faces a historical repetition of issues that have presented themselves from time immemorial, albeit with the potential for more dire conse-quences should a negative outcome be realized now.

This book will detail two-sided considerations that we face today, some of which are synopsized as follows:

- Are wars inevitable? Are wars necessary? Are wars a product of good or bad intentions?
- Can humankind be expected to improve through evolution, or are we doomed to forever repeat history?
- Why do economies have extreme fluctuations (in the sense of "feast or famine")? Can economies be stabilized or, in the least, be moderated? Will the poor remain with us in every civilization to come?

- Why are there so many forms of government (including some that vie for power within the same country) at different times in the history of a nation? Is there one form that is more prone to stabilization? Do voters (choice makers) have a sufficient understanding of underlying and long-term consequences to make informed choices?

- The twentieth century was considered the "American Century." Can the United States hold that position?

- The United States and the United Nations have taken a stand on climate change. Are variations in climate attributable, in whole or in part, to human activity? Or does the current tide of belief, whether valid or not, take into account the natural cycle of temperature changes as seen throughout history and prehistory?

- What, if any, are the negative consequences of attempts to control ecological changes that some say is the result of fossil-fuel consumption? Does the US perspective take into account the impact that the disappearance of cheap energy might have on the populations of developing countries? (The cheapest are coal and wood, both carbon-dioxide producers.)

Some fingers point to population growth, which often leads into the subject of birth control. But direct efforts to control births would be futile; they run counter to basic human nature (witness the increasing world population). Goals for controlling world population can be achieved indirectly, however. Denying cheap energy and imposing mandatory environmental controls that restrict the use of effective pesticides are now scourging poorer parts of the world by creating unaffordable prices for food and allowing insects and parasites to wreak havoc and spread diseases among their populations. All of these are real human costs that are being paid to support theoretical suppositions. Are they on the bad side of poorly considered decisions? And why are they overlooked? Could it be because there is no immediate and dramatic impact on Western society? Do power brokers consider the survival of babies of Chinese, Indian, African, and Latino women when they mandate their choices? Is environmentalism the new authoritarian religion of the powerful? Driving electric cars may make us feel good and allow us the self-deceiving illusion that we're helping the environment, but it does not compensate for fossil-fuel-gulping private jets and marinas full of boats (not to mention the fact that the electricity used to power electric cars is produced primarily by burning coal)!

For those of a theological mind-set, the conundrum remains as to whether God's creation is meant to serve humankind or whether humankind is meant to serve the environment. And, if the latter is the case, will the have-nots bear the burden and pay the highest price for protecting the environment? Is humankind always the despoiler, and is modern technology the enemy?

CHAPTER 1

Knowledge

• • •

One theological concept posits that "holiness" encompasses the attributions of eternal knowledge and eternal life that are separately and distinctly reserved for God. Therefore, holiness is not inherent in humans.

In the beginning, God created the heavens and the earth (Gen. 1:1). Human life made its earthly appearance in paradise (Garden of Eden) in the form of the two innocents, Adam and Eve (Gen. 2:8–24). Subsequently, Eve and then Adam ate of the forbidden fruit of the tree of knowledge of good and evil (Gen. 3:6). As a result, the two human beings of God's creation were banished from paradise and punished (Gen. 3:16–19).

What was it about Eve's transgression that warranted such a harsh punishment—that stripped away the innocence of God's only "very" good creation? (Gen. 1:31).

The answer has been the subject of inquiry for thousands of years. Here is one thought I propose: Some religious thinking has posited that God's uniqueness (holiness) consists of eternal knowledge and eternal life. We are told that there was another tree in paradise, the tree of life (Gen. 2:9).[1] Had God not acted, and instead allowed Eve to go on and eat of the fruit of the second tree, she (and Adam) would then have acquired the requisites to be holy (eternal knowledge and eternal life) and would have become competitors of God (Gen. 3:22–24). So goes the story.

Fast-forward to the twenty-first century. Since the appearance of *Homo Sapiens* two hundred thousand years ago, progress toward achieving eternal knowledge (a virtually unattainable goal)[2] moved forward at a snails pace, progressing only in bits and pieces. Every century appeared similar to the century that preceded it. Then, in the relatively short period of the past few centuries, a geometric expansion of information—including knowledge of the universe in which we live together with knowledge of ourselves—sprang forth. Not surprisingly, just a few individuals led the charge.

The most difficult concept for us normal folks to internalize (and to behave in accordance with) is that we don't know what we don't know.

> *The Fatal Conceit (a pretense of knowledge) is to demonstrate to men how*
> *little they really know about what they imagine they can design.*
> —Nobel laureate Friedrich Hayek (1988)

---

1 These two trees are representative of the two great desires of humankind—the desire for immortality and the quest for omniscience.

2 Very few humans are capable of developing awareness beyond that allowed through our five senses. A few modern examples of humans whose cognitive powers eclipse those of others are Newton, Galileo, Einstein, Planck, Oppenheimer, and Fermi. Because of our common sensory limitations, there is universe of events happening of which we are unaware —hence our limitations of knowledge.

EDUCATION VERSUS LEARNING

As early as the twelfth century, the recognition that human and societal progression were hampered by failures to integrate the various humanistic and scientific disciplines into a core learning process
was put forth by Maimonides (1135–1205). Maimonides practiced as
a court physician in Fustat (near Cairo) in the mornings and would
mentor a few students during the afternoons, but only to those who
came to him with prior demonstrable scholarship in multiple disciplines. His was an early recognition of the philosophy of the great
minds of the Enlightenment.

The great thinkers and philosophers of the Enlightenment were
developing the concept that the advancement of civilization was
hampered by the fragmentation of disciplines, and would only move
forward when knowledge became connected. That short period of the
Enlightenment came to an abrupt end due to the French Revolution,
with its mantra of "Liberté, Egalité, Fraternité" ("Liberty, Equality,
Fraternity"). That new "civilized" philosophy became highly regard-
ed, and a model to emulate—not unlike the politically correct level-
ing and sameness pursuits that are in fashion today.

The "new" philosophy became the death knell of the Enlightenment
by stunting advanced thinking. Attempting to equalize a society in
which the constituents are not equal in intelligence, skills, emotions,
and learning abilities was (and is) counterproductive to evolutionary
progress. Not many have the genetic capability to perform with the
skill of a Van Cliburn or similar prodigies, nor are many of equal
intelligence or learning capacity. Those who do have superior capabilities advance all. It is postulated that had two hundred particular
persons never lived, humanity would still be living in caves. Political

Correctness dumbs down society and frustrates individuality and human potential.[3]

Most of our modern higher-education curricula have become specialized and fragmented. This fragmentation of learning is spurred by students needing to focus on the shortest paths that will create opportunities to make money. The traditional liberal-arts education that asked, "What is good in life, and how should I live it?" (which fostered critical thinking and character building) has yielded to research agendas. Having made this generalized observation, I recently learned of a new "ingathering of disciplines" curriculum that is being introduced by the University of Pennsylvania (and others) that addresses the shortcomings of a specialized and fragmented education (not unlike the approach used by Maimonides in the 12th century).

---

3 The political correctness culture currently in fad is a misguided challenge to free speech that is used as a technique to control language and actions that might offend any particular group of people. Political Correctness, in its most simplistic manifestation, produces a society of acceptance and conformity. Its most powerful tool is intimidation. It is antithetical to Americans' founding principles of freedom of speech and freedom of expression. Its worst manifestation is upon society, moving it from one that is centered on the rights of the individual to one that is centered on the power of government to control even the most fundamental parts of our lives. It is a shift of power from the people to the government. Historically, when that happens, a nation becomes a society that is increasingly dependent on government, with a relatively small number of elites in control. (The single most effective way to move power from the people to the government is through the health-care system [see chapter 25]).

CHAPTER 2

Who (or What) Has Had the Most Impact on History?

• • •

FIRST CONTENDER

What would someone who lived in the twentieth century say if asked who had the most impact during that era? Would the answer be Roosevelt, Churchill, Hitler, Stalin, the Pope, or someone else? Could less commonly known figures and events have had a greater influence?

Further, what role did the "-isms" of the twentieth century (Communism, Nazism, Capitalism, and Socialism) play against the concept of democracy? Do those political prescriptions have meaning to the evolved human psyche, or are they simply convenient titles for group identification? How do they compare to the concepts of individual liberty versus governmental control?

What role did politics play versus economics? Or are they the same thing? And when in the twentieth century did the pieces come together to form the genesis of today's world?

At the start of the twentieth century, a new dawn followed the Industrial Revolution and the stirring of new social movements that, in part, had their inception more than a century earlier during the French Revolution (1789–99). Promise was in the air. World expositions boasted of progress. Then, on one afternoon in Sarajevo in June 1914, the teenage assassin Gavrilo Princip fired two shots that opened Pandora's box, exposing the failings of modern and civilized societies to cope with governments gone mad.

With Princip's assassination of Archduke Franz Ferdinand of Austria, latent nationalistic stirrings were aroused that would result in the deaths of sixty million people (2.5 percent of the world's population) in World War I. As if that weren't enough bad news for humankind, the resulting Treaty of Versailles (1919) formed the basis for future devastating eruptions beyond what the anachronistic deal makers of that treaty could foresee. World War II, the Holocaust, the Cold War, the ill-conceived division of the Middle East, and their consequences are traceable to the decisions and mandates reached at Versaille.

World War I consumed the lives of so many combatants that colonial powers needed to engage in massive recruitment of soldiers of color from their colonies. Those soldiers were firsthand witnesses to the leadership weaknesses of the colonial masters that governed them. As a result, World War I and its treaty forever destroyed whatever global confidence might have existed in believing that Europe was the bastion of world order. The myth of white European superiority ended, the the world moved away from colonialism and the stage for future terrorism was set.

Is Princip a contender for the title of the person who had the most impact on the twentieth century?

SECOND CONTENDER

Other than the event at Sarajevo, who or what else might lay claim to have had the most influence on the world of the twentieth century and thereafter? Was it Alexander Fleming's discovery of penicillin, the atomic age, the moon landing, the invention of the Internet or something else?

I posit that the United States' declaration of war against Germany on April 6, 1917, had the most influence on events for the rest of the twentieth century, and far beyond. It is highly probable that, without the intervention of the United States, the Allies (England, France, Russia, etc.) would have lost the war or, at best, would have had to seek an armistice that would have favored Germany (instead of the other way around). If such were the case, there would not have been a Treaty of Versailles that demanded prohibitive reparations from Germany, and that required that Germany admit the absurd lie that it was solely responsible for the outbreak of World War I (the "War Guilt Clause"). Germans saw that clause as a national humiliation and, if nothing else, it stirred a resentful consciousness among them that would pave the way for Hitler's ascent to power.

CHAPTER 3

Why Is Peace So Elusive

• • •

There we were, trying to achieve miracles and reduce the world to what it cannot be.

—The Count-Duke of Olivares (1645)

We are never so defenseless against suffering as when we love.
—Sigmund Freud

Most cultures and religions seek peace. Yet in the history of civilizations, there has never been a protracted period of worldwide peace absent of wars. Given all of our peace-seeking rhetoric, why is peace so elusive? Why are wars lurking around every corner? Perhaps the answers lie in the basic, evolved nature of humankind.

Is humankind good or bad? Are both states absolute values? What is good, what is bad, and what determines good or bad? The good-versus-bad decisions apparently rest in the hands of humankind, whose pronouncements waver with circumstances and time. Consider that those determinations have been conditioned by our evolution which was not under our conscious control. Given all of these variables, how reliable is humankind and, by extension, society? How predictable are we for either the good or the bad?

Evolutionists tell us that our genes are in control, and are somewhat modifiable by circumstances ("survival of the fittest"). But survival of what? Are we genetically programmed to survive as whole organisms, or are our genes programmed simply to provide for their own survival by reproducing themselves within our next generation? If this is the case, it would provide the answer to why life, before the intercession of modern medicine, lasted just long enough for humans to reproduce and pass on their genes.

That may also be the answer to why humans evolved without living long enough to mature their emotions to a level that would allow harmonious living beyond the minimum life-span of genetic propagation (see chapter 7).

Every living species (human beings, animals, plants, germs, etc.) has evolved so that its host organism could survive to reproduce the next generation of its genes. Therefore, each species of life varies in life-span in accordance with its genetic code determination of puberty.

Many forms of life other than *Homo Sapiens* have evolved to have different, often superior, sensory capabilities to those of humans because they needed those particular senses to allow them to survive to the point when they could pass their own genes into subsequent generations.

Humans are generally thought to have only five senses, and, even within those five senses, our sensory input is limited.[4] Consider the expanded band of wavelengths heard by dogs—or things seen by

---

4   Edward O. Wilson, *Consilience: The Unity of Knowledge* (New York: Vintage Books, 1998). The means by which sensory input responds to our environment is through a process within our chromosomes that is referred to as "epigenetic information." As Wilson writes, "Primary epigenetic rules [prepared learning] are the automatic processes that extend from the filtering and coding of stimuli in the sense organs all the way to perception of stimuli by the brains."

insects that are not visible to the wavelengths available to humans. (The eyes of the mantis shrimp, for instance, can detect more than a dozen colors, whereas human eyes can discern primarily only three primary colors: blue, red, and yellow.) Humans are limited because evolution has provided all that is required for our survival into the next following gene-hosting generation, and nothing more. In other words, evolution is thrifty (or miserly) in not providing anything more than is actually required for genetic survival in any given natural environment. Or is it?

Sensory input and genes have a "proprioceptive" (that is, biofeedback) related relationship that allows modifications over periods of time. Is it possible that some humans (Albert Einstein, Max Planck, and others) have evolved ahead of the pack and have expanded the usual five senses to six or more senses that allow them to sense details beyond the reach of the "laggards" of the rest of humanity?

With rare exceptions, most animals seem to be able to survive throughout their genetic lifetimes without destroying their own species. Most insects, for instance, seem to have compatible community living within their own species. Would we be less self-destructive if our sensory input were expanded so that we had better comprehension of the universe in which we live?

As we are now, what is it about human beings that is such a self-destructive and radical departure from other life-forms (see chapter 4)?

War

• • •

The cannons thunder...limbs fly in all directions...one can hear the groans of victims and the howling of those performing the sacrifice—it's Humanity In Search of Happiness.
—Charles Baudelaire

War is an integral part of human nature. The use of military force might be controlled but never banished.
—Andrew Marshall, former director of the Pentagon's Office of Net Assessment

Chapter 3 begged the question, are wars inevitable? And if so, why? People have been asking these questions for ages.

Based on History 101, there is little reason to believe that humankind can remake a pattern of behavior that has hardly changed in our entire existence. History is replete with the ups and downs of war and peace. Why has humankind not figured this out and learned the lessons of history? Is it prudent to perpetually attempt to "reinvent the wheel"?

*Those who cannot remember the past are condemned to repeat it. Repetition
is the only form of permanence that nature can achieve.*

—George Santayana, philosopher

Since humankind has been on a geometric upswing in knowledge for more than a hundred years, it is apparent that the ability to acquire knowledge is not to blame in our failure to learn survival skills from the experiences of history. Then, what is the culprit? What is it that turns humans into the aggressive animals that we are?

*You can't say that civilization don't advance, however, for in every war
they kill you in a new way.*

—Will Rogers, humorist (1929)

Although human intelligence and, to a much lesser extent, our physical bodies are witness to evolutionary progress, there has been little or no change in our emotional ability to overcome the draining knowledge of self, chaos in our world, and the depressing awareness of our own mortality. These emotional shortcomings underlie the societal and political failures of human existence.

The Bible makes no mention of a "tree of emotions" in the Garden of Eden. Was that was an oversight of the Maker in creating the miracle of life? It would seem that emotions were hung out to dry without benefit of evolutionary progress. If that is so, then it may be the reason that human emotions have not matured since the days of the Neanderthal. Such lack of emotional development carries the baggage of the incapacity of societies to cope with a knowledge of self-failings and the awareness of surrounding chaos.

We shall not grow wiser before we learn that much of what we have done was very foolish.
  —Nobel laureate Friedrich Hayek, *The Road to Serfdom (1944)*

If war represents the failure of emotions to evolve, war will persist until humankind is no longer on earth (a highly probable prospect, although not necessarily as a result of wars (see chapter 34).

Si vis pacem, para bellum (If you want peace, prepare for war).
  —Publius Renatus, *De Re Militari*, fifth century AD

Let him who has no sword sell his garment and buy one.
  —Luke 22:36

Society has a need to lay blame for failures such as war and poverty. We point our fingers at governments, banks, or simply other folks who may be immigrants and/or of different races, religions, nationalities, and so forth. Historically speaking, there is nothing new to report in this dismal repetitive cycle.

The most shocking fact about war is that its victims and its instruments are individual human beings, and that these individual beings are condemned by the monstrous conventions of politics to murder or be murdered in quarrels not their own.
  —Aldous Huxley

The bottom line is that we are products of our failed evolution, and nothing—not the United Nations, academia, or religious teachings—will ever alter or change our basic desires for money, power, or fundamentalist fervor, the underlying causes for wars. We appear to be incapable of learning lessons from our thousands of years of human history and repeated failings. Wasn't World War I believed to be "the war to end all wars"? What could justify any expectation that the future will be different? Nothing could, but our hope inevitably triumphs over experience.

Finally, can straightforward diplomacy be a realistic alternative to war? Are all controversial issues resolvable through diplomacy or compromise? Note what President Lincoln had to say about the unresolved issues between the United States and the Confederacy:

> *Between* [the Confederacy] *and us the issue is distinct and inflexible. It is an issue which can only be tried by war, and decided by victory.*
> —Abraham Lincoln (last war message to
> Congress, December 6, 1864).

Despite all of the above, humanity still yearns that: *They shall beat their swords into plowshares, And their spears into pruning hooks; Nation shall not lift up sword against nation, Neither shall they learn war anymore* (Isa. 2:4).

CHAPTER 5

Mortality

• • •

We think of animals in the wild as not having knowledge of their impending death. For the most part, these same animals rarely engage in genocide. Their "kill" tendencies, with very few exceptions, are reserved for use against other species as a necessity for survival.[5]

Humans are probably unique in having knowledge of their mortality. What are the ramifications of such knowledge, whether overt or subconscious? How does humankind handle that unique knowledge?

> *The most distinctive qualities of the human species are extremely high intelligence, language, culture, and reliance on long-term social contracts. In combination they gave early Homo sapiens a decisive edge over all competing animal species, but they also exacted a price we continue to pay, composed of the shocking recognition of the self, of the finiteness of personal existence, and of the chaos of the environment. These revelations, not disobedience to the gods, are what drove humankind from paradise* [the Garden of Eden].
>
> Dr. Edward O. Wilson, *Consilience* [1998])

---

5 Chimpanzees are one of the few exceptions in that they, like humans, also murder their own; this characteristic of their species is independent of any human contact. Therefore, can the proclivity of both humans and chimps, having that same self-destructive characteristic, be linked to a similar flawed evolution (see chapter 3)? Cross-species analysis reveals the evolutionary roots of that similar behavioral trait; chimpanzees and humans share 99 percent of their genes.

Is awareness of impending death, either conscious or subconscious, an instigator to counterproductive behavior? Is that awareness a cruel trick that motivates us to seek the favor of a Creator? And, if so, what form would it take - religion, cult or any other form of group collectivism?

In his 1973 book *The Denial of Death*, Dr. Ernest Becker argues that most human activity ultimately concerns the denial of one's mortality. Therefore it is not surprising that so much of human history concerns the eternal search for the proverbial fountain of youth, and that major youth-prolonging industries flourish today in cosmetics, plastic surgery, and fashion, all of which seek to hide or deny the fact of the inevitable human process of aging and growing old.

All things considered, there is security and comfort in being part of a group—especially if that group thinks of itself as being favored in the eyes of a Creator. The downside of such a group response is that it is too easy to fall into the trap of developing a mentality of exclusivity that judges other groups as not being favored by the Creator. When this happens, we witness the rise of nationalism, racism, religious intolerance, and so on. In an extreme manifestation, groups can come to believe that they will engender favor in the eyes of the Creator by eliminating those groups who are not favored by the Creator. That's when genocide becomes the redemptive raison d'étre of it's pepetrators. As the noose was being tied around the neck of Adolph Eichmann, he stated that future generations would thank the Nazis for the genocide that they had perpetrated.

Herding (being part of a group) is not limited to animals in the wild. As a simplistic example, the next time you are approaching multilane tollbooths on a toll highway, note how often drivers get in line behind other cars, even when other lanes remain empty. Our instinctive response is to seek the security of the nonthreatening group environment of the line of cars.

There are other forms of insulation from mortality—pursuing power, accumulating wealth beyond measure, womanizing, building and naming edifices for oneself, and, in some cases, becoming a self-described do-gooder[6]—all of which are counterproductive and demeaning. The Buddha philosophized that the divestment of material things was necessary to achieve peace.

> *When All that You Ever Wanted Isn't Enough*
> —Title of a book by Rabbi Harold Kushner

> *I never wanted anything until I actually had it.*
> —Ascribed to Rabbi Jonathan ben Zakkai

Many people feel the need to create images of themselves that will lead to their salvation. They become do-gooders. Unfortunately, in many cases, the good that they believe that they are doing is merely self-serving nearsightedness that fails to take a global perspective into account. Examples include the following:

* Creating cash giveaways by essentially printing more money to "help" the poor. While there certainly are cases where such aid is justified, diluting the value of existing currency by creating and distributing "fiat dollars" will

---

6 The concept of "good" is addressed in chapter 6.

ultimately harm the poor more than any other economic class.

* Creating endangered-species protections at an economic cost, in terms of lost jobs, for those who need to support their families. The endangered-species advocates' love of creatures surpasses their compassion for their fellow human beings. Meanwhile thousands of species regularly become extinct naturally, with no human involvement.

All of the above notwithstanding, there is a real possibility that scientific and medical advances could eventually render humans physically immortal, believe the unbelievable or not. The numbers of centenarians worldwide increases every year. At the very least, life expectancies will most likely continue to be multiples of current levels. Many human organs have already been "scaffolded" and propagated with stem cells.[7] It may not be long before science will be able to replicate all organs. (The impact on society of such advances is considered in chapter 34.)

---

7 *Scaffolding* is a process whereby cells of a patient's own organs are inertly stored for future use; this eliminates any concerns for rejection, should the need for organ replication or cell replenishment arise.

CHAPTER 6

God

• • •

A knowledge of the existence of something we cannot penetrate, of the manifestations of the profoundest reason and the most radiant beauty— it is this knowledge and this emotion that constitute the truly religious attitude; in this sense, and this alone, I am a deeply religious man.

—Albert Einstein

If you live in Israel and you don't believe in miracles, then you are not a realist.

—David Ben-Gurion

The intuitive mind is a sacred gift and the rational mind is a faithful servant. We have created a society that honors the servant and has forgotten the gift.

—Albert Einstein

From time immemorial humans have grasped the smallness of themselves and how few days were given to them, even if they were fortunate enough to live long enough to die naturally. In order to assuage their discomfort about this unsettling knowledge, they created physical entities to which they attributed powers beyond their own. They created multiple variations of the entities and assigned them supernatural attributes and individual domains of control and power. These entities took the form of many gods in the heavens, which could be visualized in the form of idols.

The Bible relates that one man, Abraham, had the vision to understand that if there was a supernatural power, it could not be partially empowered (as would be the case with many gods sharing control), but rather had to be an incorporeal Unity that was beyond the ability of humankind to visualize. Abraham further knew that such a Unity was beyond any qualities associated with mortals; this Unity, to use a later phrase, could not be comprehended in anthropomorphic expressions. Thus began what became the three monotheistic organized religions of today.

Again, religions are groups that are susceptible to the same failings of any group. Hence, human strife, including wars, has often been associated with religious zeal, especially when religion becomes hijacked by politics and manipulative leaders.

We all craft theories to rationalize our daily lives. Ultimate truths, which may be painful, fall victim to our need for self-gratifying experiences in life. We create our own truths. In that sense, we each create our own versions of God whose truth is merely a reflection of our own respective truths. Does that make each of us an "Intelligent Designer"?

Humans are neither good nor bad. There is no intrinsic goodness. Within any religion, morality is a genetically derived collective illusion that turns its adherents into good cooperators. What someone might perceive as intrinsic goodness is merely a reflection of a society that has evolved its own mores or religious values for adaptive purposes. Without such values, there is no guidance to tell us that the murder of Abel by his brother Cain was either right or wrong (Gen. 4:8).

Everyone believes in God. Even professed atheists and agnostics do; they simply haven't defined the "god" that they believe in and, so, they shun the term "God." Referring to a "Supreme Power," "Intelligent Design," or other such allusion is simply a rejection of the customarily conceived anthropomorphic God that is associated with some organized religions.

Can a thinking person accept a God in which one can believe? Here are two responses:

- The Pope, a prominent theist; his trust (faith) in the existence of God is problematic.
- Stephen Hawking, a prominent atheist; his "scientific" conclusion that there is no God is also problematic.[8]

Because the anthropomorphic God depicted in some religious texts does not fly with some thinkers, they reject all concepts of God without delving further. Such non-believers may reason as follows: God is not "He"; God is not "good"; God doesn't have hands to reach out to us; God does not sit on a throne and have a white beard; God is not compassionate.

---

8 Chapter 3 posits that evolved humans lack sufficient sensory input to be aware of that which exists.

Then, what is God? The answer is that God is the Great Mystery, but certainly not something or someone with human qualities (which is the only recourse for many when they reflect about God).

> *If there is a God, no human can effect to know his mind, so what good is there in trying to enforce belief?*
> —Thomas Jefferson

Jefferson's quote notwithstanding, we humans continue to search for our identification with God even though, all the while, we know that our search will not be rewarded (except that it may produce a positive effect within each of us). Although we understand that we cannot fathom God, we feel obligated to continue the search. For many, this takes the form of extensive reading of some of the great minds who have written on the subject and, occasionally, experiencing an epiphany. In that sense, this eternal quest represents the intellectualization of an existence without a basis for belief, because believing in God implies an expectation of the nature of God, for which there is no answer. Atheists and agnostics might accept such a concept of an incomprehensible God: a concept that could refute certain religious practices.

On the other hand, if one believes that the Bible is the literal truth, that is sufficient reason to believe in the existence of God without any consideration of who, what, when, or how. In order to argue that case, consider the following:

Reality: Every year since life began, almost every species has reproduced in almost equal proportions of males and females. While such a reproduction pattern supports the continued propagation of a species, is it truly possible that the approximately fifty-fifty ratio has recurred, without fail, throughout history? Any statistician will tell you that this situation is not "possible," as it defies the laws of probability.[9] Could divine intervention be at work here? Is the "impossible" ratio proof of the existence of God?

More reality: Astrophysicists tell us that the universe is the product of four fundamental forces—gravity, electromagnetism, and strong and weak nuclear forces that were determined in less than one millionth of a second after the big bang that generated them. If any one of those values and their ratios to one another were altered, then the universe could not exist. If the ratios had been off even by as little as $1(10)^{17}$, no stars could have formed. That is just one of the many mysteries to ponder when considering creationism versus evolution.

To understand how infinitesimally small a ratio difference of $1(10)^{17}$ is, consider the following: If baking a successful cake requires one teaspoon of sugar to one cup of flour, the cake

---

9   2014 world average; 205 females for every 100 males – World Health Organization (male/female ratio)

would fail if either of those quantities were increased or decreased by a factor of 1.00000000000000001.

The bottom line is that, because of our limited evolutionary abilities, the mystery might never be solved. Perhaps God (or the "Supreme Power," for atheists and agnostics) intended for the mystery to remain unsolved.

CHAPTER 7

Emotions

• • •

We are all shaped by the accumulation of every choice we have made in our lives, as if by a sculptor. And the sculptor is us.
—James Dines, Editor, *The Dines Letter*

Emotion is a reactive process that manifests within categories that are variously characterized as anger, disgust, fear, pleasure, surprise, and so on. Any conscious reaction draws upon memory and is influenced by a myriad combination of degrees of emotion. Thus, our reactions to any scenario may be weak, strong, mixed, or new.

Emotions influence how we respond to our environment and daily encounters. Therefore, what we do (rather than what we say) more accurately reflects our individual intelligence, knowledge, and, especially, mental stability. People, more often than not, will act on their beliefs, regardless of what they say.

Emotions are reflected in facial expressions or body language. Those outward expressions can be closely imitated by acting. Genuine outward expressions can be achieved by inducing emotions that are aimed to create a desired expression (smiles, for example). An emotionally induced smile originates from a different portion of the brain than a contrived smile. The difference is detectable. The art of acting is more convincing when the artist is capable of inducing emotions within a performance, rather than simply mimicking outward expressions; the former is what is known as "method acting."[10]

Rational thought (which, perhaps, is a misnomer) is always a prisoner of emotions and cannot free itself to engage in pure reason: No one of us is Mr. Spock. So, paradoxically, scientific and other reasoned advances arise from minds that are incapable of pure reason.

Emotions are either primary (they are instinctive or inborn) or secondary (they arise from personal events):

Primary: There has been little or no evolutionary change (see chapter 4) in such emotions. They involve no conscious activity other than in reaction to genetically preprogrammed behavioral responses brought about by some elementary stimulus. Loud noises and other surprises are examples of the type of stimuli that evoke preprogrammed behavioral responses such as heart-rate and breathing changes

Secondary: These are superimposed on (and mitigate) primary emotions during everyday personal events. Examples include the joy felt over getting a promotion that settles into relief from temporary anxiety, the sadness felt upon hearing about an old acquaintance's death turning to sympathy for the family, and so on. Secondary emotional responses vary with the degree of significance of the scenario.

---

10 I am indebted to Dr. Edward O. Wilson for his insights into this complex subject.

Emotions set the tone for what folks call *meaning*, that is, the perception of meaning occurs when our brains are excited by a conscious scenario that engages our emotions.

Decision-making occurs through the competitive selection of scenarios; with the winning scenario influencing subsequent emotions. The reinforcement of our emotions and their intensity results in *moods*. When our brain generates and decides upon effective scenarios, we become *creative*.

Insanity is a result of repeated generations of scenarios that are disassociated from reality and have no survival value.

The bottom line is that the failure of humankind's primary emotions to evolve in the Darwinian sense underlies the neuroses that hinder societal progress and plague civilization (see chapter 4).

CHAPTER 8

Physical Evolution

• • •

If the eons of earth's lifetime were compressed into the span of a single year, the origin of life would have occurred at the end of January; the colonization of the land in November; the flourishing of the dinosaurs on December 15th, the evolution of mammals on Christmas day; the development of the first primates near dawn on December 31st; and the origins of man at 8 p.m. on New Year's eve. Recorded history would occupy the last 30 seconds of the last day of such a year.

—Carl Sagan

WALKING UPRIGHT (BIPEDALISM)

Physical development, as a function of evolution, is a work in progress. Primates arose from ancestors that lived in trees and are generally considered to be the first order of earthly life because their brain size is large relative to other mammals.

Humans are the only primates to move from place to place by walking upright on two legs all of the time. Other primates, such as chimpanzees, are capable of standing erect for short periods of time, but they do not travel any distance other than on all fours. Human evolution to upright movement on two legs brought about significant changes; most were positive, but some were negative.

Early humans, like these other primates, had the ability to climb trees and walk on the ground. These abilities allowed survival in diverse weather conditions and environments, including forests and grasslands.

Almost two million years ago, the grasslands in Africa began to spread; jungle became savannah. Traveling over long distances became a necessity. The thrust for survival drove evolution away from tree-climbing to bipedalism, that is, walking upright with longer strides. Walking faster over longer distances became a great advantage.

The changeover to upright movement came about through the evolution of the size and angle of the upper thighbone as it connects to the hip. The connection of the spine to the skull also had to change. Whereas the spine of chimps connects to the back of the skull so that a chimp's head leans forward, upright walkers have a spine that connects to the center of their skull so that their heads remains erect and stable while standing on two feet.

One other important distinction is important. Primates other than humans do not stand on one leg. Humans, of necessity, must have the capability of standing on one leg as a prerequisite to walking upright since there are always times when one leg is not touching the ground.

Being bipedal provides major advantages, including the ability to travel faster over long distances, reach higher, and see farther. In addition, the reduction of the human-body surface that is exposed to the sun by walking upright facilitates the regulation of body temperature.

The most significant advantage of bipedalism, however, is that it frees our hands to accomplish tasks while moving about. It may be just that advantage, that is, the ability to carry food (to a mate or offspring, or simply for storage), that spurred our survival as a species.

The above notwithstanding, there are negative consequences to being bipedal, which requires placing the entire weight of the body on just two supports (the legs). There is a skeletal price to be paid in the form of slipped and compressed disks, joint arthritis, fallen foot arches, and general back pain.

Bipedalism also requires the ability to balance by way of constant adjustment, which may decline with age. Although balancing motions (such as swaying) are most obvious when standing on one leg, they are also necessary when walking when one leg is not on the ground.

BLOOD TEMPERATURE

Warm-blooded animals have the ability to maintain a consistent blood temperature, which is an evolved characteristic of mammals and birds. In their metabolic processes, muscle energy is created via the tricarboxylic acid cycle (also known as the Krebs cycle) in which about 60 percent of the energy is transformed into heat as a by-product of the process. Warm-blooded animals have the capacity to regulate blood temperature through the retention or dissipation of that heat, retaining it through insulation (such as fur or feathers) or dissipating it through the evaporative process of sweating or panting. Shivering, which uses muscle contractions to stimulate the metabolic process, comes into play when insulation is insufficient to retain heat.

Since so much of the energy metabolism of warm-blooded animals is lost to the generation of heat, they require more food (fuel) and more frequent eating than do cold-blooded creatures such as reptiles and fish. The advantages of warm-blooded animals include the following:

- They can be active in cold environments in which cold-blooded animals can hardly move.
- They can live on almost any surface environment on the earth, including arctic regions or high mountains.
- They can remain active, seek food, and defend themselves in a wide range of outdoor temperatures.
- They are able to reproduce in cold environments.
- Their immune systems can be activated in the face of infectious threats without having to lower their body temperatures to ward off such infections.
- They are less susceptible to fungal infections, which are vulnerable to warm body temperatures.

Cold-blooded animals, on the other hand, have a lower metabolic rate and produce less heat. Therefore, more of their food goes to their body mass, and they require less food. The lesser amount of heat generated by cold-blooded animals is not conserved but is lost to the environment. Cold-blooded creatures thus take on the temperature of their surroundings. Warm environments lead to their engaging in more activity, while cold environments result in sluggishness (including hibernation, a state shared by some mammals as well). Regulating internal temperature takes the form of moving in or out of the sun, or moving to another location with a different external temperature.

The advantages of cold-blooded animals include the following:

- They require much less energy to survive than warm-blooded animals do.

- They can survive where food is less abundant.

- They can eat more infrequently than warm-blooded animals do (for example, reptiles spend long periods of time digesting).

- They can lower body temperature when food is scarce.

- They are faster than most mammals when they are warm.

- They can be much smaller than mammals and still survive (a factor of heat-loss considerations).

- They are less susceptible to infection by viruses, bacteria, and parasites because they don't have consistently warm blood to act as an incubator.

CHAPTER 9

Religion

• • •

Since we first became self-aware, our ongoing quest for meaning and identity has prompted us to ask, "Who are we?" and "Why are we here?" Those inquiries reflect humankind's deep-seated yearning to connect with something beyond our perception of our frailties. Should those inquiries lead to a religious connection through familial influence or conversion, the connection can become increasingly deep-rooted, or it can fall apart. A deep-rooted connection carries the potential to bring about religious fervor, which in turn can become a force for good or bad, even outside its own base.

> *The record of religion in the past, and tragically also in the present, has not been good. Throughout history, people have hated in the name of the God of love, practiced cruelty in the name of the God of compassion, killed in the name of the God of life, and waged war in the name of the God of peace. None of the world's great religions has been exempt from this at one point or another.*
>
> —Lord Sacks, former Chief Rabbi of England

Thousands and thousands of books and other writings have been produced on this subject. More will be written. This chapter is limited to considering a few—a very few—of the consequences to humans of our evolved need for religion.

Atheists and agnostics, on the one hand, often posit that many of humanity's ills are rooted in organized religion (see chapter 6). Believers, on the other hand, see religious learning as directed toward influencing humanity to behave in a Godlike manner (that is, one that is presumed to be good). Are the two points of view mutually exclusive?

All religious perspectives are worthy of analysis, although this examination is limited to the three Abrahamic monotheistic derivations (all of which originated in proximate geographical areas): Judaism, Christianity, and Islam.

In Judaism, the world's first monotheistic religion, history is recorded in the first portion of the Old Testament Bible, the Torah ("Law") which is comprised of the"five books of Moses." The Torah's history is a bloody story of obedience and disobedience to God and their accompanying rewards and punishments. Mosaic teachings (the Torah) goes back thousands of years prior to Christianity making its entrance on the world stage.

Christianity, the second of the three Abrahamic religions to appear, tells its history through the Gospels and a New Testament augmentation to the Bible in which an awaited Messiah (Jesus) appears. Because they share the same history, both Judaism and Christianity experienced the same trial-and-error maturing process. Were the lessons learned?

Islam, the third of the Abrahamic religions (Ibrahim in the Islamic tradition), stems from the seventh-century revelations of Muhammad (the Prophet) as recorded in the Koran ("the Recitation"). The Koran also contains references to events mentioned in the Bible, albeit with different names or different principles.

All three religions have adherents who split the basic tenets of their religions into distinct and separate sects, each with its own patterns and rituals some of which may overlap. Christianity and Islam have experienced such profound separations within their branches that some of their respective sects have historically thought of others as being nonbelievers and, consequently, worthy of damnation (the biblical "other"; see chapter 30). In recent times, however, the various belief systems within Christianity appear to have somewhat resolved their differences. Islam, being six hundred years younger than Christianity, is still in-fighting a battle that is concerned with the succession to Muhammad upon his death in 632 C.E.

No religion is immune to the consequences of the failure of human emotions to develop and mature, actions that in general are necessary for the continuation of human survival (see chapter 4).

CHAPTER 10

Money

· · ·

For all the contrivances for cheating the laboring classes of mankind, none
has been more effective than that which deludes them with paper money.
—Daniel Webster, *Congressional Record*, 1846

Government manipulation of paper money (the "fiat" money mentioned earlier) cheats the laboring classes of humankind. From May
of 2011 through June of 2013, the US Federal Reserve printed additional paper money at the rate of 13 to 20 percent of the national
debt. In general, such dilution of paper fiat money has the effect
of doubling prices in less than six years (this is correctly referred to
as "true inflation"). Think of it this way: Every six years, cut in half
whatever monies you have accumulated on which to live for the re-
mainder of your life.

Money is any item that is generally accepted as payment for goods
and services. Paper dollars are now considered to be fiat money,
because they no longer have any intrinsic value. Stated another
way, paper dollars have no backing other than faith in the government that prints them. Therefore, the value of fiat paper (its purchasing power) is at the whim of a government's political agenda.

For example, when a government finds that it needs more money than it takes in, it has several options, three of which include reducing government spending, raising taxes, or printing additional paper. Here are a few ramifications of each:

* Reducing government spending (frequently referred to as "austerity programs"): The funds for government spending in excess of government income come from borrowing. That is not necessarily a bad thing. It can bode well if the spending is used for investments that will ultimately generate a return to repay the monies borrowed. If government-borrowed monies are squandered, however, and government debts cannot be repaid, a reduction in government spending is one alternative, albeit painful, resolution.

* Raising taxes: Tax increases are a quick fix to balance a budget deficit. Raising taxes, however, reduces discretionary income, reduces spending (which, for businesses could result in job losses that reduces the tax base for subsequent periods), and creates a disincentive for productivity and investment.[11]

* Printing fiat dollars: This is another quick fix that increases the amount of paper money in circulation so that the government can spend more. The resulting diluted fiat paper money is a prime culprit in creating true inflation. What appears to be an increase in prices is, in reality, simply that it takes

---

11   The loss of jobs is directly related to punitive taxes. The near-merger of US-owned Pfizer and the British/Swedish company AstraZeneca was based on avoiding the higher taxes of the United States. Many other offshore job losses (to China, for example) are tax-related.

more diluted paper dollars to purchase the same products and services.[12]

There is no easy shortcut to restoring a currency to real backing instead of a faith-based backing that relies on the whims of government. The United States, at one time, did have dollars that were backed and secured. It was an economic system known as the "gold standard" and was based on having gold to back every dollar. The problem for the government, at that time, was that the gold standard restricted the government from printing dollars that had no backing. The system curtailed whimsical government spending and minimized "pork-barrel" giveaways by politicians trying to curry the favor of their constituents. (The issue of pork-barrel spending is discussed further in chapter 16.)

While it is possible to return to a gold standard, it would require austerity, it would be painful in the near term, and it would be politically unpopular. The short-term alternative is to keep kicking the can down the road until the country is faced with economic collapse. This strategy amounts to addressing symptoms rather than dealing with the underlying disease which is deficit spending. No household or company that cannot print money can survive deficit spending for long.

John Maynard Keynes was an influential British Socialist economist.[13] In 1922, he and Harry Dexter White, the assistant secre-

---

12 Diluting by printing robs people of their ability to survive on saved money or pension plans. With the passage of each year during inflationary periods, paper money will purchase progressively less. It is this hidden tax that is the unsettling aspect of the government's printing of paper fiat money.

13 As acclaimed business authority, Peter Drucker, noted, "Keynes was interested in the behavior of commodities while I was interested in the behavior of people."

tary of the US Treasury, influenced the outcome of a monetary conference in Genoa, Italy, that had been called to address debts that still remained from World War I. The outcome of the meeting was the creation of a short-term fix that moved world economies away from a gold standard in order to increase the global supply of money.

In 1944, Keynes and White attended another monetary conference, this time in Bretton Woods, New Hampshire, for the purpose of setting up an international gold-exchange regimen, to be called the International Monetary Fund (IMF). The IMF perpetuated the ill-conceived short-term fixes of deficit spending that have led us down the path of repeated economic crises to the present day.

Human behavior and market forces, rather than number crunching, will always dictate outcomes (see chapter 7).

> *If theory and facts disagree, so much the worse for facts.*
> —Georg Wilhelm Friedrich Hegel

After the Bretton Woods conference, White was discovered to have been actively cooperating with the Soviet Union. He died in 1948, and it remains controversial as to whether or not his involvement with the Soviets rose to the level of espionage.

Those were the folks who most influenced the economic policies of our country and the world, and whose ideas and policies remain influential among the highest circles of many governments today. Could anyone make this up?

The economic death knell of the system established at Bretton Woods was finalized when presidents Johnson and Nixon established their "guns and butter" deficit-spending economics to pay for both the Vietnam War and expanded entitlement programs.

> *If Tyranny and Oppression come to this land, it will be in the guise of fighting a foreign enemy.*
> —James Madison

In its most simplistic rationalization, Keynesian economists believe that fiat dollars promote economic health by increasing consumer-discretionary income, which will then (in their theory) promote increased demand for goods and services (read: stimulus). The government increases discretionary income through the distribution of government-stimulus money (programs like the "Car Allowance Rebate System," commonly known as "cash for clunkers") which is fueled by printing more fiat paper dollars, raising taxes, and borrowing. The burden of raising federal revenues, as described, ultimately drains those who can least afford it. Those most afflicated are the poor and the middle class who suffer from the dilution of their savings and income that comes from printing dollars to pay the interest and principal on the national debt (hidden taxes). That's the essence of Keynesian demand-side economics.

In the long term, Keynesian economics has failed wherever the experiment has been tried. The wealth that governments distribute does not result in growth, but rather feeds unproductive segments of society while reducing the incentive to invest, start businesses, and create employment. It encourages politically oriented, wasteful spending that serves to "buy" votes.

On one hand, government spending, other than for required services such as national defense, education, and other infrastructure necessities, is counterproductive to the health of an economy and to the well-being of society (see preceding paragraphs). On the other hand, government spending is well conceived if it enables future value creation by the private sector and is aligned with those endeavors that are advantageous to society. Therein lies the problem: governments, with their self-serving and politically motivated bureaucracies of ill-informed advisers, have a poor record of acting nobly in the best interests of the nation.

> *The Budget should be balanced, the Treasury should be refilled, public debt should be reduced, the arrogance of officialdom should be tempered and controlled, and the assistance to foreign lands should be curtailed, lest Rome will become bankrupt. People must again learn to work instead of living on public assistance.*
>
> —Cicero

The decisions made by governmental bureaucracies that control our lives are almost invariably political in nature (read: self-serving). Government decision-makers are shielded from the effects of their decisions on society. In other words, government bureaucracies are insulated from their failures. In contrast, private-sector decisions are focused on value creation. Failure in the private sector is fatal. Governments do not provide the wealth of a nation. That can only be accomplished through the private sector.

CHAPTER 11

Greed

• • •

Squirrels store nuts to last for short periods of deprivation. Some humans store money far in excess of the needs of their entire remaining life. Some humans rob and cheat unnecessarily. For what purpose do humans behave this way?

Evolution has created greed as a basic element of human nature. That's good! Within limits, greed is the motor that propels innovation and productivity. Unbounded greed, however, takes other nefarious forms: the ruthless acquisition of money and power, overblown perceptions of prestige, womanizing behavior and societal and religious snobberies and repressions.

> *What is greed? Of course, none of us is greedy. It's only the other fellow who's greedy. The world runs on individuals pursuing their separate interest. The great achievements of civilization have not come from government bureaus. Einstein didn't construct his theory under order from a bureaucrat. Henry Ford didn't revolutionize the automobile industry that way. In the only cases in which the masses have escaped grinding poverty...in recorded history are where they have had capitalism and largely free trade....There is no alternative way, so far discovered, of improving the lot of the ordinary people that can hold a candle to productive activities that are unleashed by a free-enterprise system.*
>
> —Milton Friedman

Do people on their deathbeds wish that they had spent less time with their families so that they could have spent more time engaged in making money? Unfortunately, the realization of misguided priorities frequently comes too late and, suddenly, money becomes of little value.

Is there a subconscious drive that leads us to believe that excess money will stave off death? At the very least, the greed that spurs material accumulation appears to have somehow created a subconscious illusion that money can buy time.

Would human behavior change if people knew the exact date of their death?

There are those who associate capitalism with greed, especially among Socialists. They are puzzled by the fact that capitalism has elevated the economic status of all people, especially the have-nots (see chapter 12 for more on this issue). The answer to those who are baffled by this apparent paradox is that capitalism succeeds not because it is based on greed, but because the freedom to trade and do business with others is in harmony with our evolved human nature. To paraphrase Adam Smith, evolution has hard-wired us for freedom.

The Poor

• • •

Regardless of the wealth of a nation or a community, the poor have always been with us. Charity, as a concept, would not exist if that weren't so.

Witness the multitude of social programs that have not been able to elevate the poor to the next-level social stratum of the middle class. "Middle class" is defined herein as folks who must earn wages to meet their financial obligations and who do not need financial assistance. They are self-sufficient. They have enough because they earn enough. They may not have enough for savings or recreation, but they pay their bills with the fruit of their own efforts. If they reach the level of having sufficient surplus earnings to afford the extras, they are elevated to the upper-middle class.

It has been posited that if all the wealth of a nation were divided equally among the populace, those who were poor and those who were wealthy would revert to their former status within a relatively short period of time. Why is that so? Excluding disabilities, both physical and mental, the answer must lie somewhere in the emotions that control skills and aggression. Intelligence does not appear to be the major mover.

It is easy to say that there are the rich and the poor and so something should be done. But in history there are always the rich and the poor. If the poor were not as poor we would still call them the poor. I mean whoever has less can be called the poor. You will always have 10% that have less and 10% that have the most.

—John F. Nash, mathematician and Nobel laureate
(the subject of the film *A Beautiful Mind*)

Professor Harry Frankfurt writes in his book, *On Equality*, that there is a "dangerous conflict between equality and liberty." Frankfurt's view is that leaving people free to choose their work and how they decide to live will always lead to an unequal distribution of wealth. To be otherwise, that is, to eliminate inequality would require government intervention in free choice, which would equate to meddling with liberty.

Simply defined, "poor" is generally thought of as having few resources (lack of accumulated wealth and goods). Exceptions to that definition are those who disdain materialism—Mother Theresa, Mahatma Gandhi, the Buddha, monks, and others who take a vow of poverty (and who do not consider themselves as being "poor"). Considering the lack of possessions of both groups, it would appear that being "poor" is a state of mind.

What is it that can lead members of the same family to remain (or become) poor while others achieve higher levels? Is it laziness? Is it fear of failure? Is poorness inherent in individuals? Can failure (which is a judgmental value) be induced or exacerbated externally?

For many people, work is a rewarding experience, irrespective of remuneration. Work is an ethic that derives from societal and familial expectations and takes the form of employment or self-employment. There are other influencing forces, however, that may alter that perception of work; they include boredom, an unpleasant work environment, ill-tempered employers, and intolerable co-workers.

Whether we leave our homes to go to work in the morning or work at home, almost everyone must work to generate income to acquire the products that we need for survival. Physical survival requires food for nutrition and protection from the environment (clothing and shelter). Mental and emotional health adds to physical well-being and longevity. Work that is pleasant, intriguing, and conducive to a sense of productivity and satisfaction fosters mental health and a sense of purpose. It factors into a sense of validation for one's own life.

When Adam and Eve were expelled from Paradise (the Garden of Eden) because of their transgressions, the punishment for Adam was that he would have to earn his sustenance through his sweat until he died (Gen. 3:16–19; also see chapter 1). Whether one believes in creationism or evolution, it appears that obtaining food for survival necessitates work.

Suppose that evolution went another way, and that human survival was not conditioned on having to work for food. Suppose that human bodies, like plants, could simply absorb nutrients from their surroundings without putting forth any effort. Even clothes or housing might not be a necessity if life were spent in a warm climate. What would life be like under such circumstances?

I posit that life would be miserable. Work, rather than being a biblical punishment for sin, is a blessing. What would the meaning and purpose of life be if not to be productive? Where would we find the joy of discovery? What would be our validation for being alive? Why would I have written this book?

Substantial numbers of people feel that retirement from work is over-rated. Many of those who enjoy their work opt to continue working until they are no longer physically able to do so. Others, who find that their work has changed into something less rewarding, retire and later find that their sought-after retirement is less rewarding than they had envisioned. Perhaps we were not meant to live into a retirement age that has been extended by modern medicine. In this extended "scenario" (as I used the word in chapter 7), we have lost some of the meaning of life that came with our working years.

Self-perception is all too often a barrier to change, because we humans tend to allow outside influences to shape our thoughts of ourselves. We relegate to external shaping forces our perceptions of our own personal successes or failures when, in fact, our state of mind and being are the products of internal qualities such as ability, character, appearance, and health. Positive-image folks tend to preserve outside influences because they attribute their own successes to those outside influences. Negative-image folks want changes because they attribute their fail-ures to those outside influences. Both types employ self-deception about outside influences to justify either a positive or negative image, but, in reality, both types are shaped by their internal qualities.

Entirely separate from any individual's own internal disincentives to work are governmental incentives to *not* work. In other words, aside from the natural forces that foster poverty, government subsidies tend to cultivate and exacerbate welfare mentalities (see chapter 13). For example, in states that have reduced the eligible time period in which people can collect unemployment benefits, employment rose when the benefits ended. The message is clear; folks are less prone to find available employment so long as they can continue to collect unemployment payments.

When Pat McCrory became the Republican governor of North Carolina in 2013, the unemployment rate in many rural towns stood at 20 percent. Under McCrory, the state chose to not accept additional federal benefits that required repayment. Instead, he introduced the following reforms:

- Reduction of personal-income-tax rates.
- Reduction of corporate tax rates.
- Elimination of all estate taxes.
- Rejection of "free" payments from the federal government to extend unemployment benefits.
- Reduction of the length of employment benefits from twenty-six weeks to twenty weeks
- Reduction of weekly unemployment benefits from $535 to $350

Not unexpectedly, the Republican administration was lambasted for being cruel and making North Carolina a crucible for extremism and injustice. The media went on to charge the administration with cutting taxes for the rich while slashing benefits for the poor. What really happened?

- Business conditions in North Carolina went from a low of forty-fourth in the country in 2013 to being sixteenth in the country in 2015 (according to the Tax Foundation's State Business Tax Climate Index).

* $2.8 billion in unemployment insurance that was owed to the federal government was repaid; North Carolina now has a surplus.

* Employers witnessed an eighteen-month, $500 million reduction in state and federal unemployment taxes.

* State revenues went up 6 percent in 2015, generating a $400 million surplus.

All of the above factors led the Wells Fargo Economics Group to claim that "North Carolina's economy has shifted into high gear. Hiring has picked up across nearly every industry." This kind of progress happens when farsighted governments recognize that humans have evolved to respond to incentives. Here are a few lessons we can learn from cases in point:

* Paying people not to work reduces the incentive to seek employment.

* Government extensions of unemployment benefits merely extends the disincentive to seek work.

* Businesses reduce hiring because they have to compete with unemployment benefits that, in order to attract workers, they would be compelled to offer above-market wages to induce workers to forfeit their benefits and return to work.

* In 2014, one million jobs were filled by those who elected to find work after their benefits were exhausted. Those folks would not have sought employment had their unemployment-benefit extensions been continued (National Bureau of Economic Research).

The irony is this: The federal government takes credit for the one million new jobs when, in fact, it was the government itself that perpetuated the continuing unemployment of those same one million workers through the extension of their unemployment benefits.

It doesn't take much for folks to come to think of government as a cornucopia. An electorate that favors an ever-expanding big government imagines a state that is different from one that can remain viable in our economic world. Many voters will never understand the reasons they struggle with low-wage jobs. Income inequality has become the political cause célèbre of left leaning politicians in their pursuit of fairness when, in fact, their method of pursuing income redistribution simply widens the gap.

Apart from inheritance, people become wealthy through education, investment, business building, or hard work (and, frequently, all of the above). It is these folks who develop products and services and create jobs, which results in "good inequality" because it enriches the wealth of a nation. Without the economic growth that stems from the "movers and shakers," income inequality would cease to exist—we would all be equally poor.

To illustrate the point, consider the following: Which is better for everyone, a system in which everyone makes $20,000 per year or one in which 99 percent of the people make $50,000 per year and 1 percent makes $1 million per year? The first scenario will eliminate envy and divisiveness, but not much else!

Unfortunately, there is another route to wealth: government cronyism, which creates "bad inequality." This includes those few who get rich through the exploitation of government favors. It also includes fat-cat bureaucracies that get progressively fatter and exist to a large extent primarily to throw a continuous stream of money at failed government initiatives. These include counterproductive aid programs for the poor (one of the more egregious was Lyndon Johnson's flawed War on Poverty which created a dependent mentality that uprooted nuclear families). All too frequently, the root of income inequality points directly at government misguidance that widens the income gap.

As conservative columnist Jeff Jacoby wrote in the *Boston Globe* (November 30, 2014), "The most significant driver of that income inequality—the biggest impediment to upward economic mobility—isn't hard to identify. The higher the fraction of children not being raised by their married parents, the more of our fellow citizens for whom the American Dream is likely to remain beyond reach."

THE EFFECT ON MARRIAGE

The War on Poverty declared by President Lyndon Johnson in 1964 has had little positive effect on poverty in America, but it took a major toll on marriage. The so-called Great Society programs that grew out of the War on Poverty included food stamps, Medicare, Medicaid, Head Start, educational funding, and housing assistance.

Devon M. Herrick, senior fellow at the National Center for Policy Analysis (NCPA), wrote, "Ironically, the Great Society legislation seemed to simultaneously both ignore—and hinder—the most effective antipoverty program: marriage."

Around 1970, about 84 percent of native-born 30 to 44-year-old Americans were married. By 2007, the percentage had dropped to 60 percent. For those without a college degree, it dropped to 56 percent, and for Black women, to 33 percent.

The proportion of Americans living in poverty today is about the same as it was in 1966, two years after the War on Poverty began. How has the United States' efforts to deal with income inequality and fair-share distribution played out?

Income equalization is the target goal of progressive taxes and wealth-redistribution agendas. Simply stated, it amounts to higher taxes for higher earners and the sharing of such bounty with lower-income earners. Data for 2011 from the Congressional Budget Office (CBO) indicate that the implementation of such sharing has had the following effects:[14]

* The top 1 percent of earners funded 24 percent of all government expenditures.
* The lowest 60 percent of earners received more in government benefits than they paid in taxes.

Given the above revelation, the "fair share" cause falls on its face as a nonissue. Politicians play the envy card against the unfamiliar faces of businesspeople (who are easy to hate) while, at the same time, they overlook the familiar faces of entertainers and sports figures (whom the voters love).

If, as French economist Thomas Piketty wrote in December of 2014, "wealth inequality is currently much less extreme than a century

---

14 As reported in the *Wall Street Journal*, November 24, 2014.

ago," what triggered such progress? Was it redistribution of wealth, as is the cause célèbre of Progressives? Was it the sharing of wealth through charity? Perhaps the concept of inequality itself needs to be reexamined. For that undertaking, the role of the commonly denigrated "1 percent" must be reexamined.

There is no shortage of major charitable foundations. What is the source of their wealth? To use the Ford Foundation as an example, the money came from producing products that both enhanced life (cars) and delivered goods to consumers (trucks). Both benefited the economy, reduced costs, and created jobs. In doing so, "mover and shaker" Henry Ford personally elevated himself from the lower echelon of society into the top 1 percent. Having reached that point, Ford fed into a popular perception of inequality, but, at the same time, he made everyone better off.

A more current example is Larry Page, the CEO of Google. Page has an estimated net worth of $30 billion. Without Google, society would be poorer to the tune of trillions of dollars in commerce that is attributable to Google searchability, e-mail, and maps. Many other such examples can be drawn from the real world.

Perhaps Progressives should stop focusing on entrepreneurs' wealth and, instead, focus on the value that society gains from their products and services. Inequality is not a dreaded factor in capitalism; rather, it is a feature that improves the lot of all of society. Society cannot be economically elevated if it eschews the reality of inequality.

> *A rising tide lifts all the boats.*
> —The New England Council

If readers accept the premise that economic improvements help all of society, then, perhaps, the focus of charitable foundations should be directed elsewhere. In lieu of giveaways, would society be better served if the efforts of charitable foundations would concentrate on reducing barriers to business formation and cutting the massive regulatory chains that inhibit hiring, both within the United States and globally?

Can we evolved humans give up the fun of boasting about how righteous we are in our simplistic cause of challenging income inequality when we demand, *Down with income inequality—meanwhile, public welfare be damned?*

According to Fr. Robert Sirico, president of the Acton Institute, writing in response to Pope Francis's 2015 encyclical "Laudato Si" (roughly translated from medieval Italian as "Praise Be to You"), "Capitalism has spurred the greatest reduction in global poverty in world history: the number of people living on $1.25 per a day fell to 375 million in 2013 from 811 million in 1991, according to the International Labor Office. This is only one statistic among reams of evidence that vindicate capitalism."

According to Arthur Brooks, president of the American Enterprise Institute, in 1938 one in four people in the world lived on less than one dollar per day. Today, the advance of trade and a globalized economy has shrunk that figure to one in twenty. Capitalism has liberated hundreds of millions of people from desperate poverty; this is one of the world's greatest success stories, and it remains largely untold and unheralded. Capitalism has saved a couple of billion people from poverty, and we treat this miracle like a state secret. We should be shouting it from the rooftops. The growth of market freedom will liberate ever more millions from the bondage of poverty and despair.

Governments that promote capitalism do not view the poor as liabilities to be managed by government. Rather, the poor are human beings with untapped potential.

> *Beethoven took a page from Friedrich Schiller's "Ode to Joy" and incorporated it into his Ninth Symphony: "Beggars become Princes' brothers." If this is so, it can only be because of free enterprise."*
> —Arthur Brooks (paraphrased)

Income inequality is not what should be at issue. The real issue is the disposable income of lower earners. From the inception of the federal effort to "correct" the income-inequality gap, the middle class has become worse off. Though this effort is well intentioned, the net result has been to reduce the disposable income of those very people whom the government's inequality programs were supposed to help.[15]

What does it matter if the income-inequality gap appears to be reduced, if the beneficiaries of such fairness suffer through having less income at their disposal because of such efforts? (For the impact on an economy of printing money and progressive taxes see chapter 10.) Government efforts to reduce inequality should be redirected to increasing opportunity and prosperity for the benefit of all. Instead of wealth being redistributed, Americans would like to earn more income! A word of caution: the well-meaning tendency to overreact

---

15 In the two-year period ending in 2011, the middle class suffered an average reduction of its disposable income of almost 2 percent, while, at the same time, prices were rising. Such a reduction of disposable income does not bode well for families or the larger economy.

may put society itself at risk. As the Bible puts it, *"Do not show partiality to the poor or favoritism to the great"* (Lev. 19:15).

In conclusion, like wars, the poor have been with us throughout the history of civilization. There is no reason to expect that the situation will be different in the future. Because of the variables of personality and emotions in human nature, the existence of a poor segment of will continue to be a constant in every society. Understanding that, it is societys' reaction to their poor that is the measure of a society.

"A country isn't a rock. It's not an extension of one's self. It's what it stands for when standing for something is the most difficult!" (from the film *Judgment at Nuremberg*).

CHAPTER 13

Charity

• • •

But how shall we expect charity towards others, when we are uncharitable to ourselves? "Charity begins at home," is the voice of the world.
—Sir Thomas Browne

But if any widow has children or nephews, let them learn first to shew piety at home, and to requite their parents: for that is good and acceptable before God.
—1 Timothy 5:4

An anecdotal story tells of a conversation between Justice Oliver Wendell Holmes and Justice Learned Hand. As they parted ways, Hand said to Holmes: "Do justice, sir, do justice." Holmes replied, "That is not my job; my job is to apply the law."

One result of the current polarization that is taking place in America is the challenge to politics vis-à-vis the poor. Politics is invariably associated with laws. The question is whether or not laws represent justice.

Justice is not law; Justice is what is true, correct, fair, and inspired by love.

—Anonymous

Inscribed on the cornerstone of most Reform Jewish temples is this admonition from Micah 6:8: "Do Justice, Love Mercy and Walk Humbly with Your God." As profound as these words are, it is the order of the commands that is significant. The ancient prophets apparently recognized that social justice took precedence over compassion, humility, and ritual religious observance.

From the end of World War II until recently, Americans have prospered beyond all expectations. Along with that prosperity came a cult-like belief in the growth of government, and that the government should be the primary source of aid to the poor. The attraction to big government coincided with the growth of the dumbing-down protectionist concept that folks are too frail to compete in American society (also known as *political correctness*). The concept that government should be the primary source of aid to the poor—is not supported by historical or religious tradition.

The biblical mandate is to help the "stranger, widow, and orphan" (Exod. 22:21–23). That mandate is coupled with the mandate for anonymity expounded in Leviticus 19:10: "And you shall not glean your vineyard, nor shall you gather every grape of your vineyard; you shall leave them for the poor and the stranger: I am the Lord your God"; this admonition refers to anonymous gathering when no others are nearby to witness the event. Biblical law mandates that charity must be coupled with anonymity. Both conditions must be met before an act of giving can be considered charity.

Traditionally, private groups have been the major source of charity via multiple self-help organizations (such as family, the Salvation Army, houses of worship, and community associations). The critical distinction between self-help and government aid is that, unlike community self-help groups, government aid almost inevitably creates malignant dependencies in which government beneficiaries develop a state of mind that they are entitled to wealth that has been created by others.

There is a small segment of society whose disenfranchisement can only be helped through government intervention (such as people with certain mental and physical disabilities that require institutionalization and disabled veterans). That has always been the case. Many Americans, however, have come to believe in a massive redistribution of wealth through the growth of government and the government's power to tax and borrow. Those folks are unaware of their own history (or have forgotten) the previously mentioned biblical admonition, "Do not show partiality to the poor or favoritism to the great" (Lev. 19:15).

Consider the decades of the 1940s and 1950s, when so many intelligent well-meaning do-gooders were enamored with Communism. They believed that their hearts and minds were in the right place. What they were lacking was the wisdom of a global perspective that embraced the American capitalistic system (with all of its flaws) as being better than any system in the history of the world. They were searching for something new when they already had the best in their own backyard.

We are now witnessing a return to a misguided mentality that is discarding a system proved to have been the most beneficial to the entire world in every aspect. Are proponents of this anachronistic mentality taking us back to the thinking of the 1940s and 1950s? The direction that we seem to be heading will give the twenty-first century to someone else, and all because of the mismanagement of our national treasure.

The above notwithstanding, those who will come to lead are obligated to attempt to mitigate the damage to the poor that will result from misguided politics. We can divide these efforts into effective or ineffective traditions and values. The effective traditions and fundamental values include

- private *lending* to others, to help them to "get back on their feet,"
- private *giving* to those who will never be able get back on their feet without assistance (donor and receiver should remain unknown to each other),
- voluntarism, and
- creation of a society that minimizes poverty and the need to address it (which is not within the scope of this chapter).

Ineffective methods and policies include

- borrowing in order to give to others, especially if repayment is improbable, which will destroy both the lender and borrower (especially when government is the borrower);
- laws that selectively choose others to pay for aid to the poor, which is not charity; and
- anything that diminishes human dignity, causes embarrassment, or leads to an entitlement mentality that damages society (especially when government is the enabler).

Is the federal government relying on a Ponzi scheme to fund its "charitable" entitlement programs?

In 1920, Charles Ponzi immortalized his name with a scam to make wealth by creating a pyramid in which those at the top would grow wealthy with monies taken from an increasingly larger base of capital contributors. The scheme did not incorporate making profits to create wealth. As those at the bottom rose toward the top and the pyramid became larger, the scheme became more dependent on an ever-increasing amount of new capital contributors starting at the bottom. As expected, when the base of new contributors started to whither, the pyramid fell apart.

The modern-day poster boy of the Ponzi scheme, Bernie Madoff, will spend the rest of his life in jail for his shenanigans. Many were hurt, including legitimate charities, who allowed themselves to be duped by the delusion of unrealistically high returns.

In 2012, the liberal writer Ben J. Wattenberg wrote an op-ed piece in the *Wall Street Journal* called "What's Really behind the Entitlement Crisis." Wattenberg attributed the looming entitlement crisis to the issue of insufficient new births. What he meant was that the bottom of the pyramid was not growing fast enough to support the top. He said that "the real danger is too few births" (China will be the poster nation for their ill-advised population control shenanigans).

It is apparent that the federal government took a lesson from Mr. Madoff. The difference is that Mr. Madoff is in jail!

Republicans are often perceived as being for big business at the expense of the poor. In general, Democrats believe that government should care for the poor, whereas Republicans believe that the private sector can do a more efficient job. In many communities, individuals and self-help groups will invariably aid those in need (few have gone hungry in immigrant American communities that stick together).

> *Give a man a fish, and he eats for a day. Teach a man to fish, and he can feed himself for life.*
>
> —Chinese proverb

This is the message that is being passed on here: Words mean what people think they mean. In the United States, "liberal" has come to mean the politics of an expansive government and a welfare state. If the status of the poor has remained stagnant or declined with the expansion of entitlements, why does government persist along that failed path? Can it be that left-leaning politicians see a dependent electorate as their voter base to perpetuate their political careers? Shame on them!

Socialist (Keynesian) economic theory has morphed into the current new liberalism, which is not effective in the long term in any sense, and for good reason. Socialism is a failed economic experiment that has been the ultimate undoing of too many countries. Included among these countries are the former Soviet Union, Cuba, Argentina (the second richest country in the world in 1910), Venezuela, much of Europe, and North Korea compared to South Korea (both equally devastated economies in 1953).

It is obligatory to treat the poor sympathetically and non-judgmentally. In doing so we must adhere to effective values and traditions and not blindly ignore what history teaches us. Serious observers must consider this question: Has it been government largess or has it been capitalism that brought more people out of poverty? In other words, is it dependency or capitalism that raises the wealth of us all?

CHAPTER 14

Nationalism

• • •

Nations are extended tribes that exhibit all of the successes and failings of tribes: physical security for the group, pride, common and measurable mediums of exchange, common language, common culture, and heredity (but not always). Those are some of the positives of being within a tribe.

Nations inevitably come upon hard times due to natural events (disease, droughts, famine), the economic squander of natural resources and national treasure, and, most importantly, poor leadership. It is in such times that the underdeveloped emotions of human beings come to the surface. In such times, events frequently lead to internal anarchy or efforts to rob other extended tribes. And these circumstances are called war—civil or foreign.

CHAPTER 15

Government

• • •

—generally the best thing we can do to make the world a better place is-absolutely nothing. In most cases the best outcome will happen if government gets out of the way and lets people pursue their own needs, interests and pleasures. That's because most change in most areas of human endeavor come from people just doing their thing, not by design.
Matt Ridley." *The Evolution of Everything,*

As young children, we are completely under the domination of our parents. They dictate every aspect of our lives. As children, we trade our freedoms for security. We have no choice.

Later, as we grew older, we often rebel and, in response, our parents occasionally allow us some choices.

When we finally become independent of our parents, we enter a world of freedom—or so we think. Government insidiously substitutes for our parents. We don't realize or think about it; it becomes normal. Instead of relying on restrictions imposed by our own parents, the government takes over that role.

We have no say (other than by voting) over how much the government takes away from our earnings in taxes. We can't engage in certain activities without a license from the government: driving a car, engaging in certain occupations, restraining ourselves from actions that the government defines as criminal; some of these actions, such as abortion, are arbitrarily considered to be legal or illegal. In certain emergencies, the government can completely take away our liberty, such as conscripting us for military service.

These are merely a few of the issues that a society relies upon government for in order to have security. Individual freedom is the trade-off for that security. Security and freedom are conflicting value concepts. Excess security deprives individuals and businesses of freedoms and incentives. Excess freedoms lead to anarchy. Successful societies compromise both to achieve a workable balance.

An involvement in politics is the only way to maintain a balance of those values, even if limited only to informed voting. America's founding fathers recognized the dangers of government and power. Accordingly, they produced the Constitution as the law of the land for the United States to protect individuals from their own government.

> *They who can give up essential liberty to obtain a little temporary safety,*
> *deserve neither liberty nor safety.*
> —Benjamin Franklin

> *Americans are so enamored of equality, they would rather be equal in*
> *slavery than unequal in freedom.*
> —Alexis de Tocqueville

Most of the world—including American citizens—thinks of our country as a democracy. The fact is that the Constitution of the United States defines our form of government as a republic. The distinction is significant. Although it is more complex than this, a simplistic distinction is as follows:

- Democracy—Rule by majority decision.
- Republic—Rule by law and due process.

The 1943 movie *The Ox-Bow Incident* portrays the distinction. According to the story, a posse captures three men and accuses them of being horse thieves because the horses that they were riding had the brand of recently stolen horses. The posse, under pressure from their leader, refuses to accept the three men's explanation that they had just purchased the horses (from the real horse thieves, who were caught later). The posse votes, and the three are hanged.

The plot of the movie depicts democracy in action, which is majority rule. If the posse had conducted themselves as mandated by our Constitution, the three men would have been brought to a court for trial and subjected to a process that law dictates: they would have had due process.

Government comes in many forms. Democracies and Republics are merely two of them. Given enough time, many governments morph into alternate forms.

The most prevalent form of government throughout history has been the monarchy. The majority of subjects did well by this system in the past: it provided security and the messianic trust (i.e., the primitive emotions) that people needed to assign to another person (namely, the monarch). A few of these subjects ultimately would find that a monarchy, with its singular decision-making abilities, was distasteful, to state it mildly. With sufficient backing a new regime would usurp power and the process would repeat itself. The changeover process could be relatively peaceful (Magna Carta, 1215) or it could be violent (the French Revolution, 1789–1799) when heads rolled.

The system of political changeover can take many forms and may take centuries. A characteristic changeover from a democracy to an alternate form frequently follow this pattern:

Capitalism ⇨ *Socialism* ⇨ *Hyperinflation* ⇨ *Depression* ⇨ *Anarchy* ⇨ *Dictatorship.*

The "Anarchy" phase is initiated when there is no more money to support a welfare state and many go hungry and can no longer feed their families. After the Dictatorship phase, the entire cycle may be repeated, contingent upon the will and strength of the people for change.

In 1787, Alexander Tytler, a Scottish professor of history at the University of Edinburgh, wrote this about the fall of the Athenian Republic some two thousand years earlier:

> A democracy is always temporary in nature; it simply cannot exist as a permanent form of government. A democracy will continue to exist up until the time that voters discover that they can vote themselves generous gifts from the public treasury. From that moment on, the majority always votes for the candidates who promise the most benefits from the public treasury, with

the result that every democracy will finally collapse over loose fiscal policy, [which is] always followed by a dictatorship.

In his *Cycle of Democracy* (1770), Tytler stated, "The average age of the world's great civilizations, from the beginning of history, has been about 200 years.

During those 200 years, these nations always progressed through the following sequence:

* From bondage to spiritual faith
* From spiritual faith to great courage
* From courage to liberty [Democracy]
* From liberty to abundance [Capitalism?]
* From abundance to complacency
* From complacency to apathy
* From apathy to dependence [Socialism/welfare state]
* From dependence back into bondage" [Dictatorship]

The above schematics are not representative of any political affiliation, Democrat, Republican, or otherwise. For human beings who are subject to any of these variations, it is the longing of collective minds for change that will bring about a replacement form. Where are we in the aforementioned schematic?

Any man who thinks he can be happy and prosperous by letting the government take care of him better take a closer look at the American Indian.

—Henry Ford

Americans bicker over entitlement spoils as the nation continues to pile up trillion-dollar deficits. Enforced equality, rather than liberty, is the new national creed. Cutting back on government goodies seems far worse than the disease of borrowing trillions (leaving the mortgage for the unborn to pay) or transitioning to the next downward phase of the above path that was followed by failed democracies.

> *Giving money and power to government is like giving whiskey and car keys to teenage boys.*
>
> —P. J. O'Rourke, *Parliament of Whores*

History has shown that a government's redistribution of shrinking wealth, in preference to a private sector's creation of new sources of wealth, can prove more destructive than even the most deadly external enemy.

> *The essence of Government is power; and power, lodged as it must be in human hands, will ever be liable to abuse.*
>
> —James Madison

Politicians and bureaucrats think that they can design everything. In essence, this is the corruption of power. When such ignorance backfires, as it so often does, they attribute it to "unintended consequences," which is their euphemism for ignorance. Why would we expect anything different? Politicians and bureaucrats rarely are experienced in private-sector enterprises where the consequence of making inappropriate decisions is *failure*. And, paradoxically, the electorate frequently rewards failures with political reelection or bureaucratic promotion.

It is hard to imagine a more stupid or dangerous way of making decisions than by putting those decisions in the hands of people who pay no price for being wrong.

—Thomas Sowell, Hoover Institution senior fellow

Asymmetric information—a term applied to regulators who have less information than those that they regulate.

—Jean Tirole, 2014 Nobel laureate in Economic Sciences

Imposing ineffective dictums via executive order or court-ordered obedience, is a way to rule, but it isn't governing.

My reading of history convinces me that most bad government results from too much government.

—Thomas Jefferson

Government is a business. It sells roads, defense, and so on, for which its citizens pay a tax. It also exacts taxes to promote ideological concepts such as abolishing poverty, which, based upon historical residence, have proven to be illusionary [do the phrases "hope," "change," "fairness" sound familiar?]. *Administrations that fail to deliver on such ideological concepts always blame previous administrations* [as justification to raise taxes].

—David Mamet, *The Secret of Knowledge* (paraphrased)

People respond to incentives. High taxes and overregulation dampen incentives. Lowering barriers for people to develop and produce goods and services fosters economic growth. The real issue for tolerating any government is to what extent it governs by mandate, and to what extent it leaves individuals to decide for themselves how to conduct their own lives. In other words, where in the following spectrum that ranges from total government control to total individual freedom will a society tolerate? The spectrum is best visualized by a scale created by the aforementioned investment analyst James Dines:

GOVERNMENT MORE IMPORTANT VERSUS INDIVIDUAL MORE IMPORTANT

The spectrum starts with number 1 (most government control) and progresses to number 10 (most individual control):

1. *Monarchy / Dictatorship / Tyranny / State reliance*: police control, total taxation, gay bashing, antiheroism versus collective heroism, gangs, *1984*

2. *Marxism / Fascism / Communism / Military junta*: racism, death penalty

3. *Cultism / Rightism / Leftism*: pro-life, high taxes, chastity

4. *United Nations / World government*: religious fundamentalism, Socialism, strictness with criminals, class warfare, high taxes, government health care

5. Strong government / Benevolent dictatorship: antitrust laws

6. Keynesianism / Democratic Party: liberalism, no death penalty

7. Constitutional monarchy: mainstream moderate, permissive toward criminals

8. Conservatism / Republican Party: no racism, mergers allowed, low taxation, promiscuity

9. Libertarianism/nationalism: John Birch Society, National Rifle Association, pro-choice, American Civil Liberties Union

10. Anarchy: gay rights, individual heroism, no price controls, laissez-faire religion

Unfortunately, after having shed blood and treasure to achieve individual freedoms, the modern trend is for citizens to lose sight of what they fought for and relapse back to the perceived security of economic and social equality. The consequences of that lapse are the loss of being able to hold on to their earnings and being able to speak their mind. That is what happens when citizens forfeit their individuality through big government's redistribution of wealth and subordination of individual rights to group rights. Such reversion gives the green light for certain groups to make self-serving demands for themselves at the expense of society at large. Individual freedoms and incentives are the victims.

—Richard Pipes (CIA specialist on Soviet affairs),
Property and Freedom (paraphrased)

The unprecedented and increasing debt of the United States threatens the prosperity of the generation that insists on squandering the greatest gift that any civilization could bestow; the blessings of liberty. Democracies that place too much value on security run the high risk of ultimately becoming totalitarian. As Madeleine L'Engle wrote in *A Wrinkle in Time*, "Security is the most seductive thing. I've come to the conclusion that [security is] the greatest evil there is."

If you want total security, go to prison. There you're fed, clothed, given medical care and so on. The only thing lacking…is freedom.
—Dwight D. Eisenhower

Historically, Communism and Fascism have been thought of as polar opposites (left and right wing) and have warred against each other. Yet, both are almost at the top of the preceding list in terms of government control being more important than individuals being in control of their own lives.

In speaking of Bolshevism [near the top of the list], *the 1904 Nobel laureate in Physiology or Medicine, Ivan Pavlov (1849–1936) had this to say:* ["[They] *will never have a real government, but only the administration of slaves.*"]
—Daniel Todes, *Ivan Pavlov: A Russian Life in Science*, 2014.

With which number(s) on the preceding scale would you associate yourself? You will likely be somewhere around the middle and possibly closer to the bottom (i.e., the inclination that people are more important than government).

This way of viewing political inclinations is the most accurate way to identify your political stance. Certainly, it is more revealing than simply attaching a party label to yourself.

One biological instinct for humans is to favor those with whom they are most intimate, that is, close friends, neighbors, relatives, and common origin (in terms of race or religion). With the multitude of variances inherent in such human interactions, there is an innate inclination to resist a one-size-fits-all conformance imposed by government.

Although the issues of individualism can never be fully resolved, a successful political order will channel those disparate individual impulses into productive and publicly beneficial ways while still respecting individual liberties. Should a government fail to administer impartially in managing the natural divisive instincts of its inhabitants, political decay will ensue and the modern rule-of-law state will decline.

The American Declaration of Independence provides that "All men... are endowed by their Creator with certain unalienable Rights, that among these are Life, Liberty, and the pursuit of Happiness." What prompted Thomas Jefferson to include "the pursuit of Happiness" along with these other rights? From the wording of the entire phrase, it would appear that Jefferson (who was a Deist) conceived that "life" and "liberty" are inherent blessings from a "Creator," but that "happiness" derives from humankind's right to pursue it. The Declaration leaves open the exact nature of the "pursuit" that will result in individual "happiness." This is where the preceding spectrum leaves open the choice of where people will find their own "happiness."

> *When the people fear their government, there is tyranny; when the government fears the people, there is liberty.*
> —Thomas Jefferson

CHAPTER 16

Politics

• • •

The US Constitution provides that members of the House of Representatives shall serve for two years, and that members of the Senate shall serve for six years; this means that every two years, on average, one-third of senators' terms expire. There are no limits to how many times any member of Congress may be reelected. Let me repeat that: *There are no term limits.* What are the ramifications of not having term limits, as applied to the solvency and life-span of the republic of the United States of America?

> *The American Republic will endure until the day Congress discovers that*
> *it can bribe the public with the public's own money.*
> —Alexis de Tocqueville

The issue of term limits applies to state as well as federal legislators. Consider a hypothetical situation in which employees within a company have salaries and benefits that are established by their employer. Further, those employees have the right to periodically replace their employer with another person of their choosing. Any employer who doesn't satisfy the employees' demands will be looking for another job! Now, consider that government is the single largest employer of voters, many of whom are members of public-employee unions. Elected legislators control the wages and benefits of those union members. Is it any wonder why it is so difficult for states to remain solvent? (Keep in mind that, unlike the federal government, states cannot print dollars.) Term limits would curb the corrupt conflict-of-interest bargain between state lawmakers and public unions that is inherent in the system.[16]

Because the issue of term limits surfaces again and again, issues related to retaining the status quo or instituting term limits are of national concern, and any change requires a Constitutional amendment.

> *There is no provision for a rotation, nor anything to prevent the perpetuity of office in the same hands for life; which by a little well-timed bribery, will probably be done.*
> —Mercy Otis Warren, American Revolution propagandist

It appears that de Tocqueville and Warren are like thinkers. The "bribery" alluded to by both de Tocqueville and Warren is a prime contributor to our national debt. Members of Congress endear themselves to the voters in their respective states by a phenomenon that came to be known as the "pork barrel" (mentioned in chapter 10). Pork barreling is the appropriation of government spending for localized projects that are secured solely or primarily to bring money to a representative's district, thereby increasing the potential for the incumbent to be reelected.

Pork-barrel spending, which amounts to politicians spending taxpayers' money to buy votes, has always been part of the American political system. Buying votes is one of the most egregious and shameful

---

16 Between 2002 and 2014, 86 percent of Illinois state lawmakers received campaign cash from government unions (Illinois Policy Institute).

examples of the abuse of power. "Pork" can be attached to a bill in several ways. It can be as a result of pressure from the executive branch, or it can be insinuated into a bill by a legislator to mollify constituents. These "deals" are taxpayer-funded and add to the national debt, for which future generations will be stuck with the tab.[17]

If you look at the history of any country that has attempted to redistribute its wealth via social engineering[18], you will find decreased levels of motivation to invest and start businesses, which results in increased unemployment and dwindling taxable incomes. Witness what happened to Argentina since the early part of the twentieth century, going from a nation whose wealth was exceeded only by that of the United States to now being one of the poorer countries of the world.

A welfare state compromises its citizenry to the extent that the political faction that uses government to distribute unearned wealth wins elections. A broke America cannot help anyone, especially the poor.

Instituting term limits would negate the need to buy votes. If incumbents could not seek reelection, their need for pork-barrel giveaways would be restrained. Asking politicians to push for term limits, however, is asking them to act against their own self-interests—never mind the national debt.

---

17 As of this writing, the national debt stands at $19 trillion. It is difficult to internalize this mind-boggling number. The author believes that such a debt is impossible to pay back, a situation that will have dire consequences for future generations. To comprehend the enormity of such debt, consider this: if $1 million had been spent every single day from the day that Julius Caesar was born (100 BC) to late-2015, the total amount would be less than $1 trillion. The federal debt is now nineteen times that amount, and growing.

18 —*social engineering schemes to make people smarter, happier or anything else are destined to fail.* Matt Ridley, *The Evolution of Everything*

> *There is little natural constituency for innovation for the future of democratic politics, where, by definition, established voting blocs and donor interests and media alliances are those that represent the past.*
> —Holman W. Jenkins, Jr., in the *Wall Street Journal*, November 29, 2014.

The congressional annual salaries and perquisites include (as of 2014) the following:

- Members of Congress: $174,000 plus expenses, cost-of-living adjustments (COLA), and travel to home states
- Speaker of the House: $223,500 plus expenses, COLA, and travel to home state
- Major and Minority Party Leaders: $193,400 plus expenses, COLA, and travel to home states

Add to the above their pension plans, which start after only five years of service; the average pension payments for the majority of congresspeople is $60,972.

Did you know that being a representative in Congress is a part-time job? Did you know that representatives are allowed to be gainfully employed and earn income from other work, such as from the practice of law, at the same time they are serving in Congress?

Is it any wonder that individual members of Congress are willing to dip into the national treasury to give away the money of others in order to encourage their constituents to vote for them at the polls? Is it any wonder that the folks who get the money tend to vote for the incumbents?

What level of patriotism would it take for selfless representatives to break that vicious cycle? What level of patriotism would it take for the electorate to vote the best people into office rather than the officials who bear gifts?

The poor are no exception to these self-interest failings. If they had the ability to not be poor, they would be the bankers, politicians, the rich, and others at whom people like to point fingers. They are poor, to whatever degree they are poor, because they don't have the ability to be otherwise; the poor will always be with us. Paradoxically, with their limited foresight, they act against their own self-interests by repeatedly supporting and voting for failed socialistic agendas and administrations. The lessons of repeated historical truths fall victim to shortsighted greed.

The above does not mean that society doesn't have an obligation to subsidize the needs of the poor where appropriate ("the widow, stranger, and orphan"). During extreme swings of the political pendulum, however, governments consume themselves in carelessly over-catering to their voting electorate.

Can there really be such a thing—that is, a situation where society consumes itself? Of course! It happens when society bankrupts itself in its attempts to indulge the demands of specific voting segments. The incentive for productivity, which is the only way to provide economic stability, is stripped away in the process. And with it goes society's ability to provide assistance to its truly disenfranchised segment. The baby is thrown out with the bathwater.

Decades after President Lyndon Johnson declared his War on Poverty the percentage of Americans ages eighteen to sixty-four who live below the poverty line rose by 30.5 percent (between 1966 and 2012, according to the US Census Bureau). What did Johnson's well-intentioned but naïve Great Society do for the poor other than increase their numbers? What did it do to our country, other than to further polarize us and increase the gap between classes?

> *"Programs that are labeled as being for the poor, for the needy, almost always have effects exactly the opposite of those which their well-intentioned sponsors intend them to have.*
>
> —Milton Friedman on PBS's *The Open Mind* (1975)

CHAPTER 17

The Constitution of the United States

• • •

The American people are complacent about the form of government that they have enjoyed since declaring their intention to break away from England in 1776. Is such smug complacency justified? Is the electorate aware of the historical democracies that eventually morphed into tyrannies? A cursory lesson in history should remove any such smugness.

The freedoms that we take for granted—speech, religion, assembly, and others—are not natural conditions of society, whether ancient or modern. They are far removed from what we would like to believe to be universal rights. Wherever those rights exist today, they came about in modern times through a series of military victories, using the Magna Carta as a model. That document sowed the seeds of modern constitutional government and the freedoms it allows.

Have many of us forgotten that the Weimar Republic became Nazi Germany? Should we take another look at the history of Cuba? The United States handled Cuban affairs of state following Cuba's independence from Spain in 1898. In 1902, Cuba became an independent republic with free and fair elections. Today (2015), it is a Communist dictatorship. Any Cuban exile can tell you about the regrettable loss of democracy, freedom, and individual rights that has afflicted that country.

Examples abound from time immemorial. Have we such a flawed evolution that we are incapable of passing on the lessons of history to future generations?

Despite the ease with which societies may lapse into tyranny, many examples surface to demonstrate that constitutional roots can germinate anywhere: witness Hong Kong in the midst of China, witness Israel in the midst of the middle-East.

Although the following quote appeared in the preface, it is worth repeating:

> *That men do not learn very much from the lessons of history is the most important of all the lessons of history.*
> —Aldous Huxley

To say that tyranny can't happen in the United States is a misreading of history! The only thing that protects us is the Constitution of the United States.

When they conceived our Constitution and Bill of Rights, the descendants of English nationals (our founding fathers) were informed by the Magna Carta, that revolutionary document signed by King John in 1215. Those eighteenth-century US documents reduced the potential of the new nation from slipping into anarchy followed by tyranny.

Then, as now, people in much of the world are subject to decrees handed down from government (or from members of the clergy who presume to interpret a holy book). Challenging that form of governing is our Constitution, which mandates that government be bound by the same rules as the most disenfranchised segment of society, and that those rules arise as laws from the bottom up—from the people—and are enforceable only through due process.

Another view of our Constitution is that its provisions were designed in a negative format; that is, that the rights of Americans were drafted as principles to prevent government coercion. That protection has come down to us in the form of the aforementioned due process wherein only laws drafted with the consent of the governed can be applied to societal conduct.

This is why we hold that federal laws are made by a self-governing people. And those laws are enacted only through a freely elected Congress (or so it is conceived in our Constitution). As visualized when the United States was in its infancy, the Supreme Court is charged with judging the constitutionality of laws created by Congress, and the role of the president of the United States is limited to administering those laws. Neither the Supreme Court nor the president is granted the authority to make laws. The American people are guaranteed that only their multimember Congress, elected and representing every state within the nation, can establish the laws of the nation. The Constitution bars any one person from becoming a tyrant for very long.

It has been said that if a frog is thrown into boiling water, it will instinctively jump out. If that same frog, however, is put into cold water that is gradually heated, it will be scalded to death. The second-frog example illustrates how tyrannies evolve. Hitler didn't become a dictator overnight. In the democratic elections of 1932, German voters gave the Nazi party sufficient strength that could facilitate Hitler moving to become their dictator. If the German people had paid closer attention to the slow erosion of their rights, culminating in the laws of 1935, Hitler could have been stopped. But few took notice, especially if it didn't affect them directly or immediately.

An activist Supreme Court (the judicial branch of the US government) or any lower court pose threats to usurping the lawmaking prerogative limited to Congress (and only Congress, per the Constitution). The president of the United States (the administrative branch of government) puts forth the same threat by utilizing executive orders in order to bypass Congress (the only lawmakers who represent the people).

While I do not presume to have the knowledge of constitutional experts, it is commonly known that the courts, and the president, are limited to interpreting law, and such interpretations become rulings to which we are all subject. We must carefully scrutinize whether or not such practices adhere to the protection of our right as provided for in our Constitution. Otherwise, the country will find itself on a slippery slope and could readily morph into a tyranny. You don't think so? Neither did the people within all of the democracies that have gone down that slippery slope. Can anyone presume to know more than our founding fathers did about the dangers inherent in any democracy when they risked their all to gift us with our Constitution?

During the Civil War, the Confederacy hid behind the issue of states' rights to mask the fact that it was fighting to preserve the South's odious perpetuation of human slavery (based on a misperceived economic need). Even today, there are those who link slavery to the South's cause célèbre of states' rights, and that is unfortunate. States' rights was a separate Federalist concept, independent of the slavery issue, that was intended to maintain the integrity of each state to govern intrastate issues through its own elected legislature independent of outside (federal) interference. It is reasonable to assume that folks on their own turf best understand local issues.

Federal mandates are too often dictated by appointed, that is, unelected, bureaucracies and agencies that are presupposed to serve the welfare of the citizenry. Unfortunately, in too many instances those bureaucracies and agencis merely serve to promote political agendas that, all too frequently, simply serve to perpetuate their own growth. One of the many dangers of governance by appointed agencies is that, unlike elected legislators, bureaucratic agencies are rarely dismantled, and their agents are rarely removed from office. There are countless federal agencies that no longer serve any purpose other than to consume taxpayer dollars and drain the national treasury. They only exist to provide a misguided sense of security for people who believe that "government knows best" what is good for all of us.

Finally, here's a repeat of key quotes in chapter 15, because these concepts bear repeating:

> *They who can give up essential liberty to obtain a little temporary safety, deserve neither liberty nor safety.*
> —Benjamin Franklin

> *Americans are so enamored of equality, they would rather be equal in slavery than unequal in freedom.*
> —Alexis de Tocqueville

CHAPTER 18

Socialism

• • •

Equality, especially income equality, has been touted as an objective in many nations. Where such experiments in income equalization have been attempted, the results have always been impoverished nations and failed states.

Democracy extends the sphere of individual freedom, socialism restricts it. Democracy attaches all possible value to each man; socialism makes each man a mere agent, a mere number. Democracy and socialism have nothing in common but one word: equality. But notice the difference: while democracy seeks equality in liberty, socialism seeks equality in restraint and servitude.

—Alexis de Tocqueville

The democracy will cease to exist when you take away from those who are willing to work and give to those who would not.
—Thomas Jefferson

The problem with socialism is that you eventually run out of other people's money.

—Margaret Thatcher

Socialism is not necessarily a bad concept. The eternally underlying issue boils down to whether people choose to live with more government or choose more individual liberty (see chapter 15). Without getting into detailed descriptions, the main thrust of Socialism aims for communal rather than individual ownership of the workings of an economy (see the de Tocqueville quote, above). The multitude of failures associated with Socialism has resulted from the impact of human foibles on the mechanism. Any "-ism" system—capitalism, Socialism, Communism, and so on—could be workable if not for the imposition of evolved human imperfections, weaknesses, and shortcomings (detailed earlier, especially in chapter 13, which deals with borrowing). Economists shortchange the imposition of humankind's imperfections when they invent their theories. They take existential particulars that are, in fact, merely symptoms and fit them to the mold of their theories. Meanwhile, the underlying disease (human frailty) remains, to surface again at any time.

> *There is no difference between communism and socialism, except in the means of achieving the same ultimate end: communism proposes to enslave men by force, socialism by vote. It is merely the difference between murder and suicide.*
>
> —Ayn Rand

When human failings are considered and taken into account, Capitalism, with all its flaws, generates a result that is least harmful for society and the world. Capitalism, as a historical economic system, resulted in the United States becoming the benefactor to the world during some of the most trying times in history. Capitalism thrives on innovation and rewards. Capitalism is fueled by people who aspire for personal freedom (as opposed to Socialism). Witness the former

Eastern bloc folks who have seen their standards of living raised after their societies were restored to free markets and individual property.

Capitalism is absolutely the worst economic system-except for all of the others that have been tried from time to time (paraphrased from a Winston Churchill statement pertaining to the Democratic form of government).

> *Capitalists believe that wealth is generated by those of imagination, vision, and strong work ethics. They believe that political power is generated by wealth. Socialists believe that political power generates wealth that is then parceled out as patronage to sustain those in power.*
>
> —Carl O. Shuster, letter to the editor, *Wall Street Journal*, November 29, 2014

Other lessons we can learn are that capitalism is the only economic system that benefits all (including the poor and the middle class), and that class warfare (singling out the "one percent," for example) is divisive and minimizes incentives for growth. Envy of others, which leads to wealth-redistribution mentalities, is destructive to both individuals and society. In the past as well as now, the majority of the top one percent started with very little and grew the country along with themselves. A few examples out of many include Bill Gates, Steve Jobs, Thomas Edison, and Henry Ford.

> *Those who benefit most from freer markets* [i.e., capitalism] *are the have-nots; those without inherited wealth, prestigious credentials, social or class advantages—in other words, people whose only hope for a better life is a social order that will reward their hard work and enterprise. Certainly, that has been borne out by the world's experience.*
>
> —Arthur Brooks, president of the American Enterprise Institute (which receives no government funding)

The reason that the United States is the wealthiest country in the world is that, historically, our culture encouraged rising into the top one percent. Look at any other country in history that punishes success (through progressive taxation, wealth redistribution, and confiscation) in the misguided name of fairness, and then choose which type of culture is better for everyone, both rich and poor.

Socialism is a sure bet to turn the "American dream" into a European nightmare. Economic theory notwithstanding, trial and error appears to be the most reliable test of the compatibility of humankind with an "-ism." That is a lesson of history; when human intellect falters and emotions prevail, the resulting governing "-ism" fails along with it. Place your bets!

The truth is that nobody really understands or has ever understood how to produce economic growth except by getting out of the way and allowing the process to happen. In the end, growth results from innumerable individual decisions and by indeterminate economic factors, each pursuing its own end. If that is greed, then it is time to recognize the power of greed to spur the growth that is beneficial to all, rich and poor.

There is no viable alternative to the dynamic, market-based economy that is capitalism. History demonstrates that no other system has ever proved to be successful at generating economic growth. Attempts by some economic experts to reinvent the wheel are futile, because there is nothing new under the sun (Eccles. 1:4–11). Even the ancients in the Bible seems to be telling us to learn from history, the only honest and reliable teacher.

According to Harold Bershady, in his book *Moving on from Marx*, poverty will always be with us. Socialism is not, and has never been, the answer to poverty. Socialism carries the destructive illusion of a messianic utopianism. Proponents of Socialism fall back on the argument that Socialism is moral. Does Socialism result in a moral society and, if so, in what way? Does it incentivize humankind and society to progress? Does it help the poor?

> *Those who favor socialism always make the moral case for it. The truth is, maybe they actually believe in it, but in the real world socialism harms it, it weakens the economies of countries that have tried it. it just does. Weaker economies hurt everybody in them. Socialism kills incentive, opportunity, freedom. It is just the opposite of what America is all about. Look, socialism always harms the people it claims to help the most. It handicaps them, leaving them weaker, less self-determined, less free. [The* case for Socialism] *is actually immoral. Spending money you don't have is immoral. Borrowing more money than you can pay back is immoral. Lying to the American people is immoral. We cannot measure success by how many people are dependent on our government.*
> —Bobby Jindal, former governor of Louisiana

The best that can be done is to create a society in which minimum government intrusion works to incentivize productivity, that being the preeminent way to mitigate poverty.

As a final note, it is a genetic human tendency to optimistically believe that change is progress. Since there rarely is anything new under the sun, progress too often is a repeat of a prior historical experiment that has been ignored. Because humans demonstrate a serious deficiency in learning from history, progress is often a repeat of a prior social experiment that failed.

How many times have we heard that there is no free lunch? Well, is that the truth or just some old idea that no longer applies in a modern socialist society? All goods and services must be paid for. The only question is, who will ultimately pay? In other words, what is the source of the wealth that must be tapped for payment? The answer, the only answer, is the source of wealth that emanates from the productive segment of a free society. Government has never been a source of wealth.

Socialism—frequently in the guise of democracy—provides a seemingly free lunch in the form of programs such as supplemental income, tax credits for unearned income, tax exemptions, tobacco subsidies, dairy subsidies, payments to not plant crops (such as the US Department of Agriculture's Conservation Reserve Program, or CRP), and entitlements, just to mention a few "freebies." Government can only give-away what it takes away from others.

> *Be careful of what you wish for, you just might get it.*
> —Anonymous

> *If it ain't broke, don't fix it.*
> —Bert Lance, businessman and former director
> of the Office of Management and Budget

As demonstrated by history, Socialist dogma is exciting but misguided. Conservative dogma is about what we should retain that made America great and how to hold onto it. Conservatives want personal liberty, individual incentives, opportunity, and free markets to preserve the wonderful dreams of the founding fathers rather than "throwing them under the bus". Most illusory do-gooder agendas are government intrusions that, paradoxically, work to the disadvantage of the poor and middle class, but retain the ability of those in office to buy votes—which they do.

Conservatism is a movement whose ideology is that good things are easily destroyed, but not easily created. The work of destruction is quick, easy, and exhilarating. The work of creation is slow, laborious, and dull. Conservatives are boring. The reality of these facts is that conservatives suffer a disadvantage in public opinion.

> *It may seem strange that any men should dare to ask a just God's assistance*
> *in wringing their bread from the sweat of other men.*
> —Abraham Lincoln, second inaugural address

Liberals are fond of raising the banner of inequality; they decry the conservative approach to government as being unfair. While fairness is an honorable aim, it is how fairness is applied that separates Liberals from Conservatives. Liberals would have government promote financial equality because we are all created equal, and, consequently, the field should be level at the finish line. Conservatives, on the other hand, believe that hard work and merit, not government intervention, should determine rewards. In other words, the concept that we are all created equal is more aptly and justifiably applied to the starting line.[19]

---

19 The Conservative approach must incorporate an effort to encourage the idea that the starting line does, in fact, provide for an equal start. That is not the case in the United States, because government intervention since the inception of the War on Poverty has resulted in dramatically decreasing numbers of nuclear families and increasing the numbers of children being raised without a father in the home (see chapter 30). Such children are disadvantaged at the starting line. Government aid, in order to be effective, must include incentives for betterment. Aid that stifles incentives thwarts evolved human aspirations and has, historically, been the downfall of many societies. In our evolved education system, segregating children by merit and intelligence has become politically incorrect (see chapter 23). An enlightened education establishment should be more focused on quality of *outcomes* rather than "one size fits all" groupings that disregards abilities.

You choose!

CULTURE WARS

Extremists in religious, cultural, political, and other movements have been at war with society since time immemorial. As patterns of societal thought evolve, the tendency is for both sides of any issue to reject extremes and moderate toward the middle, resulting in no winners and no losers. Accommodation wins.

In my early life (post World War II), American values mainly consisted of hard work, personal responsibility, individual merit, delayed gratification, social mobility, and love of country vis-à-vis the idea of "American exceptionalism".

In the mainstream mentality of the time period, men were thought of as being the breadwinners (see the "sweat of the brow" biblical mandate (Gen. 3:16–19). Indiscriminate sex, homosexuality, and women's rights (including abortion) were not openly discussed. Racial discrimination was ignored. That was the era during which I moved from adolescence to adulthood. Conservative versus Liberal and Democratic versus Republican issues seemed less polarized and divisive to the majority of Americans. If you were to ask the typical guy on the street to describe the difference between the social or political perspectives of the two political parties, he would have found it difficult to answer the question.

This mentality, considered to be conservative at the time, had a dark underside in that the disenfranchised segments of American society were brushed under the rug. But that was soon to change; a culture war was brewing. Mainstream thought came under attack. Conservatives defended their viewpoint as necessary to ensure a good future for their adherents. The Left had no sympathy for that perspective.

> *Nothing is more powerful than an idea whose time has come.*
> —Ascribed to Victor Hugo

The fight was on. The new Left sought to discredit cultural conservativism as repressive. The leftist banner was raised for women's rights; gay rights (including same-sex marriage) and expanded opportunities for minorities.

For those of us who moved to the middle ground, achieving accommodation must be the path to betterment. Accommodation must win! Middle-ground Conservatives have come to recognize that their lifestyles are not threatened by accepting diversity, while the middle-ground Left has come to understand that the Conservative mentality has its place among many schools of thought and is not necessarily repressive of society at large. The values of hard work, personal responsibility, individual merit, social mobility, and delayed gratification (especially in the age of the 401k) endure for anyone who is capable of reason.

CHAPTER 19

Climate

• • •

Modern liberalism is best understood as a movement of would-be believers in search of true faith. For much of the 20th century, it was faith in History, especially in its Marxist interpretations. Now it's faith in the environment [climate issues]. *Each is a comprehensive belief system, an instruction sheet on how to live, eat and reproduce; a story of how man fell and how he might be redeemed, a tale of impending crisis that's also a moral crucible. In short, a religion without God.*

Bret Stephens, *The Wall Street Journal*, November 3, 2015

Edward Teller, the father of the hydrogen bomb and other brilliant scientific achievements, signed a petition that stated the following:

We urge the United States government to reject the global warming agreement that was written in Kyoto, Japan in December, 1997, and any other such similar proposals. The proposed limit on greenhouse gases would harm the environment, hinder the advance of science and technology, and damage the health and welfare of mankind.

There is no convincing scientific evidence that human release of carbon dioxide, methane, or other greenhouse gases is causing or will, in the foreseeable future, cause catastrophic heating of the Earth's atmosphere and disruption of the Earth's climate. Moreover, there is substantial evidence that increases in atmospheric carbon dioxide produces many beneficial effects upon the natural plant and environments of the Earth.

If Dr. Teller is wrong and the climate variations that have been visited upon this planet since pre-history can now be influenced through social engineering, there still remains another issue that, although ignored in the chase for climate control, is of fundamental significance for humanity. On one hand, the theory of being able to control climate is a scintillating issue that grabs attention and demands the allocation of significant resources. On the other hand, directing billions of dollars for climate control while there are nations that need help with tuberculosis, malaria and malnutrition brushes aside that existential human priority. Hungry and disease plagued children don't need solar panels![20]

Looking back at the long history of mild and extreme climate variations should tell us that forces beyond human manipulation are in control. Politicizing climate only leads us to strategies with unproven benefits and unreachable goals, but very real costs to society.

Why has such a controversial issue as climate management grabbed so much attention while the long standing existing needs of so much

---

20 Aid for improved health, education and economic development is being diverted to climate issues. In India, less than one percent of the projected $100 billion world goal for climate control will be spent on preventative measures that could save 300,000 malaria deaths each year (worldwide, there are more than one million malaria deaths each year). With 1.4 million children dying from malnutrition each year, 1.2 billion people living in extreme poverty and 2.6 billion lacking clean water and sanitation, the emphasis on climate is immoral.

Excerpted from an article in The Wall Street Journal by Bjorn Lomborg, Directors of the Copenhagen Census, October 22, 2015.

of the world's population are denigrated? (The plight of 3rd world countries is further explored later in this chapter 19).

The dilemma posed is simply this; should we focus on a very real human disaster that is manageable if dealt with properly, or should we assign priority to a debatable alarm that may be false and, even if true, not within humanity's ability to intervene?

Why is the government of the United States so aggressively pursuing it's massively expensive agenda to curtail human activities that it alleges are more dangerous than all international calamities, including war? The balance of this chapter will examine this enigma, beginning with these thoughts from Nicholas Wade:

> For decades leading geophysicists resisted the idea, proposed by a mere meteorologist, that the Earth's continents had drifted. Chauvinism induced French physicists to believe for years in a colleague's supposed discovery of N-rays, which they saw as an achievement to rival the German discovery of X-rays.
>
> Such debacles raised the pertinent question of whether peer review and other safeguards are always successful in protecting science from political infection. When climatologists warn of global warming, for instance, could their political passions somehow leak into the parameters of their climate models?" (Nicholas Wade, author of *A Troublesome Inheritance: Genes, Race, and Human History*, in a review of Ian Tattersall's book *The Strange Case of the Rickety Cossack* [*Wall Street Journal*, June 18, 2015].

In his book *1984*, George Orwell posits that a government can control the minds of a gullible populace by misdirecting its attention from being micromanaged to a fictitious threat. Substitute "micromanaged" with "overregulated" and "fictitious threat" with "global warming (carbon dioxide)." Can you spell r-e-d h-e-r-r-i-n-g?

> *If climate change is a reality, then that would be a huge problem that could only be dealt with by government. It would be a heaven-sent opportunity for the left to vastly increase government control over the economy and the personal lives of citizens.*
>
> —John Steele Gordon, *Business of America*

Back in 2000, the climate experts were telling us that snow might disappear forever:

* Winters with strong frost and lots of snow like we had twenty years ago will cease to exist at our latitudes (Mojib Latif, Max Planck Institute for Meteorology, Hamburg, April 1, 2000).

* Good-bye winter. Never again snow? (*Spiegel*, April 1, 2000).

* Within a few years winter snowfall will become a very rare and exciting event....Children just aren't going to know what snow is (David Viner, Climatic Research Unit, University of East Anglia, March 20, 2000).

* Computer models predict that the temperature rise will continue at that accelerated pace if emissions of heat-trapping gases are not reduced, and also predict that warming will be especially pronounced in the wintertime (*Star News*, Wilmington, NC, as reported in the *New York Times*, March 11, 2000).

The world is engaged in an important debate that centers on climate. The issues are as follows:

* Is the earth warming?

* If the earth is warming, is it due to a natural cycle of cooling and warming?

* If the earth is warming, how much is attributable to natural cycles and how much, if any, is attributable to civilization's abuse of the environment?

> *One argument that* [alarmists] *haven't tried to make explicitly is that the US commitment to emissions reductions will actually slow down warming in a meaningful way. If you believe the climate models, the US emissions reduction would reduce the warming by a fairly trivial amount that would get lost among the natural variability of climate.*
>
> —Judith Curry, climatologist, Georgia Institute of Technology

In other words, the United States and other countries have committed to the incalculable costs that are associated with their attempts to control climate, with unlikely benefits. Further, those who are spending all of that money are putting a lot of faith in their climate model, which may be terribly flawed (see below). And, even if it is absolutely accurate, their climate model predicts any warming to be a "fairly trivial amount that would get lost among the natural variability of climate."

Earth temperatures vary in small cycles encompassed by very large cycles. One of the larger cycles appears to be twelve hundred years. That comports with reports of the Norse voyagers who ventured into North America and Scandinavian areas that today are unable to grow grapes. Yet during their voyages of discovery, they called some of those general areas "Vinland" because the climate was sufficiently warm for grapes to grow.

The latest information on earth temperatures dramatically reduces the amount of global warming that will be experienced to less than half of what was previously reported. It is reported that fifteen thousand years ago the Pacific Northwest was covered by six thousand feet of ice that rapidly melted, for which there is no explanation (no humans were around to despoil the ecology during that period).

Therefore, although the issue is controversial, it remains open as to whether this is a cycle that is being repeated and to what extent, if any, human beings (and animals) influence that cycle. Breath and flatulence, coming from the largest animal population in the history of the earth, go into the atmosphere as major contributors to global warming. Here are two facts to consider:

* Carbon dioxide is emitted by burning fossil fuels.
* Life on earth could not exist without carbon dioxide. Since 1980, the extra carbon dioxide that has resulted from the use of fossils fuel has contributed to a 14 percent increase in the amount of all types of green vegetation on the planet.[21]

In 1938, the British scientist Guy Callender postulated that warming as a result of carbon-dioxide emissions was "likely to prove beneficial to mankind" by shifting the climate northward where cultivation was possible.

---

21 Alex Epstein, *The Moral Case for Fossil Fuels* (New York: The Penguin Group 2014).

We breathe it out; plants absorb it. Carbon dioxide is essential to photosynthesis, the process that sustains plant life and generates the oxygen that human beings and animals inhale. Far from polluting the world, carbon dioxide enriches it. Higher levels of carbon dioxide are associated with larger crop yields, increased forest growth, and longer growing seasons—in short, with a greener planet.

For every hundred thousand molecules of air, only thirty-eight are carbon dioxide. The global-warming exponents say that carbon-dioxide levels have risen 35 percent in the industrial era. Even if this is true, 35 percent of nothing is still nothing, and the increase in carbon dioxide has virtually no effect.

Consider that evaporated water is a much more powerful greenhouse gas than carbon dioxide, and there is twenty times more water than carbon dioxide in our atmosphere. It is the most prevalent source of greenhouse gas of them all. Put those statistics into proportion when considering the impact of burning fossil fuels on the greenhouse effect.

Writing in the *Wall Street Journal*, Steven Koonin, Undersecretary for Science at the Department of Energy during Barack Obama's first term, said, yes, the climate is changing. And yes, humans are having an impact on the climate system, though only 1 to 2 percent of it. But he stated that most climate-change models not only missed the temperature flattening of the past sixteen years, they do not capture huge factors like oceans, water vapor, cloud formation, and rainfall.

The most reliable readings of the Earth's temperature show that it peaked back in 1998. This was not widely reported in the United

States, where the state of science reporting is dismal. But over in England, where they take that sort of thing more seriously, the British Broadcasting Corporation (BBC) created quite a stir with an article headlined, "What Happened to Global Warming?" In it, BBC climate-correspondent Paul Hudson gave a summary of the problems facing the alarmists: "For the last 11 years, we have not observed any increase in global temperatures" (*Star-Ledger*, Newark, New Jersey).

On June 24, 1974, *Time Magazine* reported that "since the 1940s, the mean global temperature had dropped about 2.7°."

> *There has been no global warming since 1998 according to the most widely used measure of average global air.*
> —Bob Carter, climate and geology
> scientist, University of Australia

> *The UN no longer claims that there will be dangerous or rapid climate change in the next two decades. Global warming stopped shortly before this century began.*
> —*Wall Street Journal*, September 5, 2014

> *Scientists have discovered methane gas bubbling from the seafloor in an unexpected place: off the East Coast of the United States where the continental shelf meets the deeper Atlantic Ocean.*
> —Henry Mountain, "Methane Is Discovered
> Seeping from Seafloor off East Coast, Scientists
> Say." *New York Times*, August 24, 2014.

Is that methane another potential source of energy?

> *Methane hydrate is a seafloor source of gas that exceeds in quantity all of the world's coal, oil, and gas combined.*
> —Matt Ridley, *The Rational Optimist: How Prosperity Evolves*

In a paper published online in the journal *Nature Geoscience* (August 24, 2014), scientists, including Adam Skarke of Mississippi State University and Carolyn Ruppel of the US Geological Survey, reported evidence that the seepage had been going on for at least a thousand years.

Methane is a potent, if relatively short-lived, greenhouse gas, so that discovery should aid the study of an issue of concern to climate scientists: the potential for the release of huge stores of methane on land and under the seas as warming of the atmosphere and oceans continues.

"It highlights a really key area where we can test some of the more radical hypotheses about climate change," said John Kessler, a professor at the University of Rochester who was not involved in the research.

If the earth's temperature peaked in 1998, is it possible that we might be in a cooling trend?

Reliability of Data

As of 2013, fossil fuels provided 87 percent of the energy consumed by the world, and that had not changed in the preceding ten years. Fossil fuels are, and will indefinitely remain, the primary source of energy for the planet. Oil is used primarily for transportation, gas for heating, and coal for electricity.

> *Although remaining at the same percentage as a source of energy, the*
> *volume of fossil fuel consumption has increased (due to increased demand).*
> *Interestingly, during this same period of increased consumption, the*
> *amount of carbon dioxide emission per unit of energy has decreased. That*
> *decrease in carbon dioxide emissions is a direct result of moving from high*
> *emissions coal to lower emissions electricity.*
> —Matt Ridley, *The Rational Optimist: How Prosperity Evolves*

Parts of our world are still without electricity. In those areas, wood remains the primary source of energy. The sad statistic is that indoor air pollution from burning wood kills four million people each year. Further, fossil fuels must be credited with reducing deforestation and preserving land for the production of food.

How reliable are the data employed by the promoters of global-warming theory? A British journalist is questioning the method used by scientists to calculate the earth's climate change; Christopher Booker writes in Britain's *The Telegraph* that climate data from stations in South America have been adjusted since the 1950s to give the impression that the earth's temperature is rising more than the original data showed. *The Telegraph* called it "the worst scientific scandal of our generation." Booker cites Paul Homewood's *Not a Lot of People Know That* blog, where Homewood compares raw data with adjusted temperatures to show that the graph trend was reversed from a cooling trend to a warming one.

Homewood checked the data on three weather stations in Paraguay and found that all three had their initial raw readings adjusted to show lower temperatures in the 1950s and higher temperatures today.

Following a report by Booker of February 7, 2015, Homewood checked more stations in South America and found the same thing had occurred there.

Scientists use these records to estimate temperatures in locations that don't have reporting stations and the data are used to project changes in overall global climate. Homewood is now looking at stations in the Arctic between Canada and Siberia. "Again, in nearly every case, the same one-way adjustments have been made, to show warming up to 1 degree C or more higher than was indicated by the data that was actually recorded," Booker writes.

Traust Jonsson, a longtime climate researcher in Iceland, was surprised to see that the revised data cover up Iceland's sea-ice years approximately four to five decades ago, when a period of extreme cooling almost wiped out Iceland's economy.

Homewood reportedly became interested in the subject because of arguments from climate scientists that rising global temperatures are causing the sea ice to melt in the Arctic. In reality, Homewood says, the melting is caused by cyclical shifts in Atlantic sea currents that bring warmer water to the area. Arctic water temperatures last peaked seventy-five years ago, when sea ice melted back even farther than today.

The following testimony was given before the House Science, Space, and Technology Committee in April 2015:

> The president's Clean Power Plan requiring "every state to meet federal carbon-emission-reduction targets would reduce a sea-level increase by less than half the thickness of a dime.

Policies like these will only make the government bigger and Americans poorer, with no environmental benefit" (Charles McConnell, former assistant secretary for the Department of Energy).

Government-produced computer models used to forecast climate changes have absolutely been shown to produce illegitimate predications. What happens when the predictions from computer models are not supported by actual data? Answer: the data are ignored or changed. One of many examples of meaningful data that go unheeded is the impact of undersea volcanic eruptions.

The following are excerpts from a recent research report issued by the Lamont-Doherty Earth Observatory of Columbia University's Earth Institute, which was funded in large part by the US National Science Foundation. The essence of the report is that there is insufficient information that can be coordinated into making any climate projections that are reliable, including civilization's role, if any, in climate changes:

> "Scientists have already speculated that volcanic cycles on land emitting large amounts of carbon dioxide might influence climate. The findings suggest that models of earth's natural climate dynamics, and by extension human-influenced climate change, may have to be adjusted." The study appears this week in the journal *Geographical Research Letters*.

Some scientists think volcanoes may act in concert with Milankovitch cycles—repeating changes in the shape of earth's solar orbit, and the tilt and direction of its axis—to produce suddenly seesawing hot and cold periods. The major one is a 100,000-year cycle in which the planet's orbit around the sun changes from more or less an annual circle into an ellipse that annually brings it closer or farther from the sun. Recent ice ages seem to build up through most of the cycle; but then things suddenly warm back up near the orbit's peak eccentricity. The causes are not clear. Enter volcanoes.

Researchers have suggested that as ice caps build on land, pressure on underlying volcanoes also builds, and eruptions are suppressed. But when warming somehow starts and the ice begins melting, pressure lets up, and eruptions surge. They belch CO_2 carbon that produces more warming, which melts more ice, which creates a self-feeding effect that tips the planet suddenly into a warm period. A year 2009 paper from Harvard University says that land volcanoes worldwide indeed surged six to eight times over background levels during the most recent deglaciation, twelve to seven thousand years ago. The corollary would be that undersea volcanoes do the opposite: as earth cools, sea levels may drop one hundred meters, because so much water gets locked into ice. This relieves pressure on submarine volcanoes, and they erupt more. At some point, could the increased CO_2 from undersea eruptions start the warming that melts the ice covering volcanoes on land?

Daniel Fornari, a senior scientist at Woods Hole Oceanographic Institution not involved in the research, called the study "a very important contribution." The study "clearly could have important implications for better quantifying and characterizing our assessment of climate variations over decades to tens to hundreds of thousands of years cycles."

Edward Baker, a senior ocean scientist at the National Oceanic and Atmospheric Administration (NOAA), said, "The most interesting takeaway from this paper is that it provides further evidence that the solid Earth, and the air and water all operate as a single system."

Cost

According to Wikipedia, the following are the costs per dollars per megawatt hours (MWh) of electricity (projected for 2019). The numbers are projections and, hence, are subject to change. Their usefulness is in their relative values to each other for comparsion purposes:

- Solar   243
- Wind (offshore)   204
- Gas (turbine)   128
- Nuclear   96
- Coal   96

In California, according to The *Wall Street Journal*, "Since 2011 solar energy has increased more than 10-fold while wind had nearly doubled. But during this period electricity rates have jumped 2.18 cents per kilowatt hour—four times the national average." Until the world accepts the benefits of nuclear energy, coal provides the lowest-cost electricity available.

Through 2016, the Obama administration will be closing down 411 plants that are producing the lowest-cost electricity in the world.[22] Prior to the election of President Obama, coal provided 52 percent of the electricity generation in our country. Today it is

---

22 The reduction of coal production, as advocated by President Obama, would result in a less than two-hundredths of a degree Celsius (0.02 C°) change in temperature by the year 2100, according to The Cato Institute (a libertarian think tank).

37 percent: all for the purpose of supporting those who stand to benefit from pursuing the idea that modern society is the cause of climate change.

We are replacing projected $96 per-megawatt-hour energy with energy that costs up to $243 per megawatt hour. And yet we claim to care about the poor and the middle class, whose disposable income is declining every year, and about developing markets that are limited to coal as an energy source?

As with all considerations, the global-warming issue should extend to the "money trail" and the "power trail" to reduce the influence of biases (human nature). There is also a religion-based bias:

> *The protection of planet Earth, the survival of all species and sustainability*
> *of our ecosystems is more than a mission. It is my religion and my dharma.*
> —Rajenda Pachauri, former UN climate scientist

Religious fervor supplants science!

Money and resources spent are ill-used for renewable energy. They have never worked efficiently (due to expenses, noise pollution and excessive maintenance). The US government already has squandered billions on research and on companies that ultimately went bankrupt. Germany is bankrupting itself on a futile commitment to wind energy that has tripled energy cost in that country and has resulted in companies relocating elsewhere.[23] When reality hits,

---

23 According to Google energy engineers Ross Koningstein and David Fork, "Trying to combat climate change exclusively with today's renewable energy technology simply won't work; we need a fundamentally different approach" (Institute of Electrical and Electronics Engineers [IEEE] *Spectrum*, November 18, 2014).

Germany will have to get its head out of the sand and go back to using nuclear power.

> *Current renewables are dead-end technologies. They are unreliable. Battery storage is inadequate. Wind and solar output depends on the weather. The cost of decarbonization using today's technology is beyond astronomical.*
>
> —Bill Gates

Further, the addition of ethanol to gasoline for the purpose of mitigating climate change is ill-conceived and costly. Biofuels made from the leftovers of harvested corn plants are worse than gasoline for global warming in the short term, challenging the administration's conclusions that they are a much cleaner oil alternative and will help combat climate change; a $500,000 Environmental Protection Agency (EPA) study funded by the federal government and released in the peer-reviewed journal *Nature Climate Change* concludes that biofuels made with corn residue prior to 2014 released 7 percent more greenhouse gases compared with conventional gasoline. Further, ethanol made from corn or sugarcane is an ecological disaster. It results in deforestation and food-price hikes, and produces more carbon dioxide than coal (per unit of energy).

The only rational weaning from fossil fuels is nuclear power. Nuclear power is being advanced by most energy-hungry areas, including France, China, India, and Russia; the exceptions are the United States and Germany. Even Japan, after the Fukushima disaster, is restarting two nuclear reactors.

> China is pushing to nearly quadruple its nuclear energy capacity by 2020. Four more Westinghouse reactors, the most

advanced design certified by the US Nuclear Regulatory Commission, are under construction in the US. Three more will be built in the UK. No country comes close to matching China's appetite for atom-splitting power. The People's Republic is currently building 29 reactors. That's four out of every 10 new plants in the world. Russia, the world's next most active nuclear-plant builder, has 10 reactors underway; India has six. Westinghouse predicts it will sell 30 reactors across the globe by 2030 as governments consider factors like energy security and pollution concerns, and as utilities weigh the steady cost of nuclear-power generation against the volatility of natural-gas prices. The US has 100 commercial nuclear reactors (in 62 plants) in operation today, but virtually all are decades old. The most recent construction permit for a new plant was issued in 1978. Given that reactors have a typical lifespan of 40 to 60 years, Westinghouse president and CEO, Danny Roderick, believes we are headed for an "energy cliff" if planning for replacement reactors doesn't happen very soon. Meanwhile China is roaring ahead (Catherine Dunn in *Fortune* Magazine, April 28, 2014).

Nuclear power would mean a liberating self-sufficiency from depending on Russia's natural gas. Nearly every nation will eventually seek to acquire nuclear power for energy independence.

The issue of nuclear waste is also hyperinflated, especially when Russian private enterprise is willing to take all that can possibly be generated. More and more countries are recognizing that trend as newer technology is introduced (our current reactors are outdated).

Paradoxically, should an anticarbon-tax movement succeed, it will accelerate the current move toward nuclear power.

> *Cuts in carbon emissions, in the form of "cap-and-trade" proposals, will raise the cost of energy, particularly electricity, and hit the poor hardest.*
> —Diana Furchtgott-Roth, *Real Clear Markets*, May 27, 2014

Americans in the lowest fifth of the income distribution spend 24 percent of their income on energy, compared to 4 percent for those in the top fifth. Electricity from solar power costs twice as much as electricity from natural gas; this, too, would raise costs and hurt the poorest Americans the most.

New costs borne by US energy producers from any cap-and-trade law would raise prices on domestic goods and allow foreign producers from countries with less stringent policies (or no policies at all) to charge less for their goods than American producers can charge. This would mean fewer jobs in the United States and more jobs offshore.

In an analysis, the EPA has proposed cutting carbon-dioxide emissions from power plants. Its ambitious pollution-control effort could force more than a third of the country's coal-fired power capacity to close by 2030, resulting in economic losses of $50 billion per year and the elimination of 224,000 jobs.

In mid-2014, President Obama proclaimed that "97 percent of scientists agree: climate change is real, man-made, and dangerous." John Kerry, Al Gore, and a host of others have championed this statistic. What underlies the agenda of the federal administration in its nonsensical claim that "97 percent of scientists agree"?

A partial answer can be found in a report produced by John L. Casey, a former White House space-program adviser, consultant to NASA headquarters, and space-shuttle engineer. He is now one of the United States' most successful and respected climate-change researchers and climate-prediction experts; he is currently (2015) the president of the Space and Science Research Corporation (SSRC). In a 164-page executive summary prepared by the SSRC for its 2013 Global Climate Status Report, Casey presents damning evidence that a network of politicians, corporations, and scientists have conspired to promote the fear of "global warming" despite evidence clearly stating that no such "global warming" exists. The motive behind the global-warming scare: $22 billion per year (the money trail).

The amount that our government pays to stop the so-called global-warming epidemic is $22 billion of taxpayers' money—that comes out to $41,856 every minute over the course of one year. That is twice as much as what our government spends on securing our borders.

This report asserts, once and for all, that global warming is a sham: a sham perpetuated by a network of government officials, greedy corporations, and, perhaps, less-than-totally-scrupulous members of the scientific community.

Suppose that the agenda of the present government were to be fully implemented whatever the price; What is the best outcome that might be expected?

As climate scientist Judith Curry of Georgia Tech testified before the House Science, Space and Technology Committee in April of

2015, "The president's UN pledge is estimated to prevent only a 0.03 Celsius temperature rise"—that is three-hundredths of one degree. The fact is that for seventeen years before that report, there has been little or no global warming. The world is 1.08 degrees cooler than it was in 1998.

The following chart represents the progression of global temperatures from 1998 to 2014:

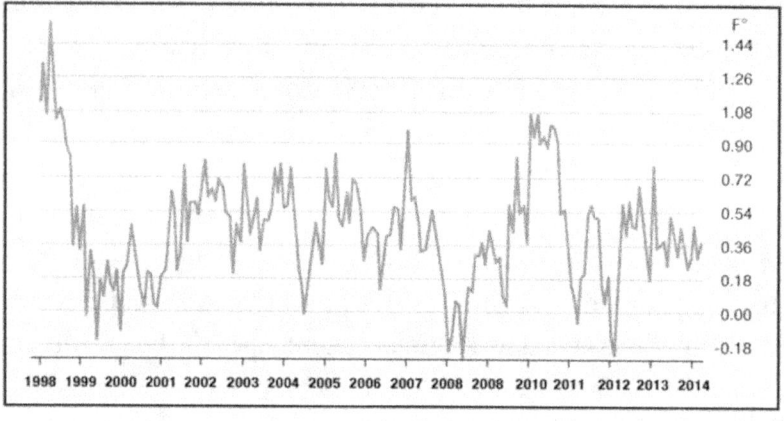

Source: NASA, NOAA and Remote Sensing Systems

The *Wall Street Journal* reported, "The assertion that 97 percent of scientists believe that climate change is a man-made, urgent problem is a fiction." When further review was done, it was discovered that a mere 1 percent of scientists believe human activity is causing most of the climate change.

Further, the earlier referenced petition signed by Dr. Edward Teller states, "there is no convincing scientific evidence that human release of carbon dioxide, methane, or other greenhouse gases is causing or will, in the foreseeable future, cause catastrophic heating of the Earth's atmosphere and disruption of the Earth's climate."

> *There is a high agreement among leading experts that long-term trends*
> *in weather disasters are not attributable to human-caused climate change.*
> —2012 Report to the United Nation's
> Intergovernmental Panel on Climate Change.

Indeed, even a founding father of the man-made-global-warming theory, Dr. Claude Allègre,[24] recently came out and renounced his position by admitting, "The cause of this climate change is unknown."

Fifteen years ago, Allègre was among the fifteen hundred prominent scientists who signed the "World Scientists' Warning to Humanity," a highly publicized letter stressing that global warming's "potential risks are very great." With a wealth of data now in, Allègre has recanted his views. To his surprise, the many extant climate models and studies failed dismally in establishing a man-made cause of catastrophic global warming. Meanwhile, increasing evidence indicates that most of the warming comes from natural phenomena. Allègre now sees global warming as overhyped and a second-rank environmental concern.

The truth is that climate change is a naturally recurring cycle (for more on cycle changes, see the earlier part of this chapter).

---

24 Claude Allègre, one of France's leading Socialists and most celebrated scientists, was among the first to sound the alarm about the dangers of global warming.

Cost to Taxpayers: Follow the Money Trail

The Solyndra green-energy initiative went bankrupt shortly after a visit by President Obama at which time the president awarded $500 million of taxpayers' money to the failing company. Here is the part of that story, along with other stories, that has been hidden:

- [1] As Solyndra fell on hard times, it passed into the hands of two large, private-equity investors, Goldman Sachs and George Kaiser. When $500 million in taxpayer money was given to Solyndra, both Goldman Sachs and George Kaiser benefited. Both have made contributions to Obama's election campaigns, adding up to roughly $1.25 million.

- [2] In 2010, another federal loan of $400 million went to Abound Solar, which also went bankrupt. But investors in Abound Solar seemed to do just fine: investors like billionaire heiress Patricia Stryker. Stryker has famously contributed $500,000 to the Coalition for Progress while throwing $85,000 toward Obama's inaugural committee. Is that another coincidence? There are many other, similar coincidences in the stories of A123 Systems, First Solar, and GE, among others.

Green energy is a very profitable business; CEOs and executives get to rake in millions of dollars, while politicians get lucrative donations for their campaigns and scientists get all the funding they need, all on the backs of taxpayers.

That $22 billion previously alluded to is just what is spent on these global-warming initiatives. The true cost includes regulations promulgated by federal agencies, such as the EPA; the shackling of free enterprise; and a forced reliance on foreign energy that *Forbes* estimates to be a staggering $1.75 trillion annually. To put that in perspective, we are wasting more than $3 million *per minute*.

We have a government that prefers comfortable self-serving delusion to uncomfortable truth.

Finally, as Edward P. Lazear, former head of the White House Committee on the Economics of Climate Change, testified, "The Obama administration is instituting a variety of far-reaching policies to reduce carbon emissions and mitigate climate change. Are any of these capable of making a difference? Simple arithmetic suggests not. Given this reality, we would be wise to consider strategies that complement and may be more effective than mitigation—namely, adaptation" (September 3, 2014).

> *Nations like Singapore, whose average daily maximum temperature is 54.5 degrees hotter than the global average, suggest that urban planning can continue to outpace nature.*
>
> —James Lovelock, *A Rough Ride to the Future*

Subsidizing wealthy conspirators to build low-density, low-output, capital-intensive, and land-hungry renewable energy schemes will rob the poor of the cheap energy provided by fossil fuels or nuclear-energy production.

> *Even in America, the contemplated closure of three nuclear plants in Illinois would have a significant negative economic impact, including $1.8 billion in annual lost economic activity and more than 7,000 job losses* (in that state alone).
>
> —Study sponsored by the State of Illinois

In conclusion, the most important consideration may be this: Events happening within our earth's atmosphere, whether human influenced or not, may be totally irrelevant due to cosmic effects. The following statements are excerpted from John Blosser's *Newsmax* article on March 11, 2015, entitled "Scientists: Orbital Variations Main Cause of Climate Change":

Global warming theorists have taken yet another hit with a new study out of Denmark which demonstrates that variations in Earth's orbit are the primary causes of climate change, and have been for at least the last 1.4 billion years.

Scientists from the University of Southern Denmark and the China National Petroleum Corporation investigated marine sediment from the Xiamaling Formation in China and determined that the sediment shows evidence that the same orbital forcing that caused the climate to change 1.4 billion years ago is the underlying force behind global warming today...

[The research findings are:] There is a wealth of evidence pointing to dramatic short-term climate change on Earth over the last few million years. Much of this climate change is driven by variations of Earth's orbit around the Sun with characteristic frequencies known as Milankovitch cycles.

Milankovitch cycles are fluctuations which occur in Earth's orbit every 20,000, 40,000 and 100,000 years, which bring about an ice age every 100,000 years or so. Currently, Earth is in the middle of a warming period, and has been for the last

11,000 years, [according to] Dr. Donald Canfield, professor at the Nordic Center for Earth Evolution at the university and one of the principle researchers...

"This research will also help us understand how Milankovitch cyclicity ultimately controls climate change on Earth," Canfield said in a statement.

The study approximates findings from a study of sea surface temperatures and diatoms, marine algae, from Aarhus University in Denmark. Researcher Marit-Solveig Seidenkrantz commented: "We know that the sun is very important for our climate, but the impact is not clear. Climate change appears to be either strengthened or weakened by solar activity. The extent of the sun's influence over time is thus not constant, but we can now conclude that the climate system is more receptive to the impact of the sun during cold periods, at least in the North Atlantic region."

[Another source reported,] "Natural forces have always caused climate on Earth to fluctuate—sometimes quite a bit. We can't control everything. The Earth is still going to orbit the sun and such orbital forcing of climate change happens over thousands of years and brings ice ages and warming periods."

[1] and [2] The information contained in the two referenced paragraphs was gleaned from usually reliable sources but not independently substantiated. Readers are encouraged to confirm their authenticity apart from the presentation in this chapter.

CHAPTER 20
Populism

• • •

The most basic definition of "populism": changes in political philosophy that favor "the people" over "the elites."

Power corrupts and absolute power corrupts absolutely.
—Lord Acton

President Richard Nixon popularized the term "the silent majority" in 1969. The term was meant to refer to an unspecified majority of people in our country who do not express their opinions publicly. In making that statement, President Nixon was admonishing Vietnam protestors by characterizing them as a vocal minority whose leanings were not supported by most people, who, although quiet, supported his continuation of the conflict.

Populism fosters giving a voice to silent majorities in that it is a movement to promote individual initiative and rights in the face of an ever-growing government that, by its very nature, moves away from individualism toward central control. The balance between individual rights and government control is detailed in chapter 15.

What though the radiance which was once so bright
Be now for ever taken from my sight,
Though nothing can bring back the hour
Of splendour in the grass, of glory in the flower,
We will grieve not, rather find
Strength in what remains behind;
—William Wordsworth (1770-1850),
"Intimations of Immortality"

Although Wordsworth's ode is not political in nature, it reflects humankind's yearning to go back to an earlier time. Populism seeks to do so as well.

In a way, Populism in the United States is a revisionist movement that would revert to the vision and politics that produced the United States of the twentieth century ("America's Century"). It is a vision for our future based on how we perceived our past; that is, Populists have a positive view of individual self-reliance and Yankee know-how. They disdain obstacles to individual empowerment. As a philosophy, Populists adhere to

* retaining, not transforming, that which made America a world leader;

* fostering progress within proven parameters, rather than making radical leaps into the unknown (i.e., learn from history);

* adhering to the American ideal of individual independence, creativity, and self-rule; and

* using the US Constitution as the governing document to promulgate societal individualism.

The desire for power is one manifestation of an evolutionary neurosis that saddles humankind (see chapter 5). If money is the root of evil, power is the root of tyranny. Power, per se, does not necessarily equate to tyranny. Power tends to be addictive, however, and the fear of its loss frequently results in a tightening of its reins and the usurpation of the rights of society. Populism is a countervailing movement.

Populism eschews collective guilt, collective responsibility, and political correctness (for more on Political Correctness, see chapter 23). Believing that most folks can run their own lives is basic to Populism, as is a rejection of government intrusion. As such, Populism periodically surfaces as a reactive movement when government becomes so concentrated that it hinders individual freedom.

Thomas Jefferson (who, ironically, owned slaves) drafted the words "All men are created equal" in the US Declaration of Independence. Clearly, "equal" means different things at different times. With all due respect to Mr. Jefferson, he might better have stated, "all people are of equal moral worth and as such deserve equal treatment under the law." As it reads in the Declaration, future generations were left to play the cards that were dealt in 1776. Leaving that statement ambiguous created the opportunity for politicians to create great inequalities in the name of "equality." (For more on equality, see chapter 12.)

Populism rejects various forms of inequality. As examples, Populism challenges

* the politically correct equal-opportunity edicts mandated by government that actually create collective inequality of opportunity. As a technique of control, political correctness

translates to reducing a population to a lower level of equal sameness; and

* the progressive movement's hostility toward income inequality (reflective of their seething resentment) that would have them curb equality of opportunity.

The recitation above is not intended to be a whitewash of Populism as a panacea. Nor is it meant to indicate, in any way, that Populism and Conservatism are twins at heart. Populism can spring from either the Left or the Right. Simply stated, Populism emerges when an established government fails to solve its most urgent problems.

To Populists, it is immaterial whether Democrats or Republicans control the seat of government if neither party responds in ways that make sense to the movement. And, because Populism identifies target villains, it offers an easy path to satisfaction. It is irrelevant whether or not the targets selected have culpability in the dissatisfaction of the movement. Outrage, whether justified or not, is one of the greatest of human pleasures. It is a manifestation of the flaw in the evolution of human emotions (see chapter 7).

Support of Populism stems from humankind's nostalgic interest in reverting to what we perceived as better times. Although that goal may be illusory, it should not be summarily dismissed. Populists' aired grievances may credibly call for a review of those aspects of history that have been beneficial for society.

CHAPTER 21

The Middle Class

• • •

A large economic middle class is an anomaly that was produced by the inflation of the second half of the twentieth century. As one example; lower-income families bought homes that were later sold at hyperinflated prices. Accordingly, with this new wealth a large part of the population went from low to middle class. The new wealth was invested into businesses and income-yielding securities that generated discretionary income. Spending the new income further fueled the inflation and elevated more segments of the population into the middle class.

> *There's nothing surer / the rich get rich and the poor get poorer.*
> —"Ain't We Got Fun," music and lyrics by
> Whiting, Egan, and Kahn (1920)

As with all inflation, the acceleration of price increases will eventually outpace the income of the new middle class, and at that point the size of the middle class will decline.

Historically, there was rarely any economic system that enjoyed a middle class as has been seen in the United States since the 1950s. It would not be misleading to state that history demonstrates that the lower income and the poor are the normal state of affairs. Utopian

"-isms," such as Communism and Socialism, have had minimal impact in changing that state of affairs. The fact is that government intrusions exacerbate the pendulum swings of economies to the detriment of stability. As one example, what benefit was derived from the price controls instituted by President Nixon?

Economies thrive on the circulation of money (i.e., spending). Is it too simplistic to say that spending requires having disposable income? If that is true, any reduction of disposable income has the potential to diminish an economy; that is, as less money circulates, businesses suffer. In turn, businesses lay-off employees and spend and less, thus creating a downward spiral. Such economies are said to be in a recession or depression (President Herbert Hoover coined the term "depression" as being a more gentle term than the previously used term which was "hard times"). (See chapter 12 for more on disposable income.)

There are two primary reasons for the squeeze on the middle and upper-middle classes:

* **Inflation**: The result of the Federal Reserve printing additional paper dollars that dilute the value of disposable income, savings, and investments. Goods and services cost more because the diluted fiat dollars used to pay for them have less value (see chapter 10).

* **Interest rates**: The artificially low interest rates promulgated by the Federal Reserve aid the government in coping with its debt. It also allows the government to increase its debt (similar to getting a larger mortgage when interest rates are low) in order to fund "pork" and other pet projects. The net effect on the middle class is to reduce any interest or dividend

income that people expect to receive from their savings (the same applies to pension plans that are underfunded because their antipated investment returns are less than projected).

Each of the above is a *hidden tax* foisted by government. Charles Schwab reports that for the six years through 2014, low interest rates resulted in an *annual reduction* of the Gross Domestic Product (GDP) by $115 billion, and seniors were receiving $58 billion less in interest income than previously. Case closed.

> *The best way to destroy the capitalistic system is to debauch the currency.*
> *By a continuing process of inflation, governments can confiscate, secretly*
> *and unobserved, an important part of the wealth of their citizens.*
> —John Maynard Keynes

To understand this historical reality, a review of the nature of humankind in earlier chapters may be helpful.

CHAPTER 22

Guns and Gun Control

• • •

The strongest reason for the people to retain the right to keep and bear arms is, as last resort, to protect themselves against tyranny.
—Thomas Jefferson

Animal and insect have evolved bodies that are effective killing instruments; they have strong teeth and jaws that can crunch bone, powerful muscles that can constrict for hours, claws that are able to rip apart muscle and sinew, poison that can be injected, and so on. In addition, animals have the ability to chase prey at high speeds; some animals have been clocked at speeds equal to that of early airplanes.

Humans are no match for the evolved killing potential of animals. What do we have instead? We have minds that can create ways to kill that are more effective than any animal mechanisms, the most prevalent of which is the gun. Not only are guns more effective, but they can kill at long range. Hooray for us!

The problem with guns is that the same human minds that created them has not evolved in its emotional maturity to restrain from unjustifiable killing, that is, murder. We thus go through repeated cycles of public debate over gun laws as we seek remedies for the extreme emotional shortcomings of a few deranged individuals.

The ebbs and flows of the "ban-the-guns" movements follow the periodic outbursts of mass violence that involve the use of guns. The fact that many mass murders are copycat responses further points to the still-primitive status of human emotions.

Despite the fact that one-on-one homicides far outnumber the deaths that have been associated with mass killings, the one-on-one murders seem to get very little attention. It is the reporting of mass killings that creates the sensationalism that titillates the emotions of the masses.

> *A well-regulated Militia, being necessary to the security of a free State,*
> *the right of the people to keep and bear Arms, shall not be infringed.*
> —Second Constitutional Amendment[25]

> *No free man shall ever be debarred the use of arms.*
> —Thomas Jefferson

---

25 In 2008, the US Supreme Court expressly ruled that the Second Amendment was intended to protect an individual's right to possess and carry firearms.

On the subject of gun-control, there appears to be no middle ground between the pros and cons:

* Advocates for stricter gun-control laws use the recurrence of mass shootings as an argument in their favor. They evoke the murders at Sandy Hook Elementary School (Connecticut), Columbine High School, and a movie theater in Aurora (the latter two in Colorado), as well as a long list of other mass shootings.

* The National Rifle Association (NRA), in contrast, leads the argument against gun control. The NRA cites the clause on the subject in the Second Amendment to the US Constitution (quoted above) as the guarantor against an infringement of the right to own guns.

An NRA mantra is, "Guns don't kill people. People kill people." That argument is irrefutable, but is it relevant to the issue of gun control?

Notwithstanding either position, has humankind's emotions evolved sufficiently to be trusted with the possession of lethal weapons? While the answer that I posit is no, I then ask how people could otherwise protect themselves or their communities in an immediate crises that could be over before the police arrive on the scene. Here are a few examples of law enforcement's inability to prevent slaughters:

* Virginia Tech, Blacksburg, Virginia, April 2007, thirty-two killed

* American Civic Association, Binghamton, New York, April 2009, thirteen killed

- Fort Hood, Texas, November 2009, thirteen killed
- Movie theater, Aurora, Colorado, July 2012, twelve killed
- Sandy Hook Elementary School, Newtown, Connecticut, December 2012, twenty-seven killed
- Navy Yard, Washington, DC, September 2013, twelve killed

According to an FBI report issued in 2014, mass shootings are happening more often resulting in more deaths and usually ending before the police get to the scene (generally, within two minutes). The report states, "Many active shooters have a real or perceived deeply held personal grievance, and the only remedy that they can perceive for that grievance is an act of catastrophic violence against a person or an institution that brings to the perpetrator a moment of omnipotent control and domination."

What alternatives might be pursued in response to the issue of how readily illegal guns, including military-type weapons, can be procured by almost anyone? Here are a few possibilities:

- Crisis training.
- Armed guards in locations where masses gather.
- Arming and training teachers or principals in the use of weapons.
- Law enforcement screening of communities for those who may be contemplating violence.
- Going on as we are—that is, everyone who is screened being permitted to own and conceal a gun (as recommended by the FBI).[26]

---

26 The media has reported interviews with people who lost loved ones in their homes, at restaurants, etc., who claimed that they could have "taken out the shooter" if only they had had a gun.

A 1982 survey of male felons in eleven state prisons dispersed across the United States found that:

* 34 percent had been "scared off, shot at, wounded, or captured by an armed victim."

* 40 percent had decided not to commit a crime because they "knew or believed that the (targeted) victim was carrying a gun."

* 69 percent personally knew other criminals who had been "scared off, shot at, wounded, or captured by an armed victim."

Colleges and universities that do not ban guns on campus have been found to have lower homicide rates than those that ban guns. It seems to follow that eliminating so-called gun-free zones and allowing teachers to carry concealed weapons could help reduce mass shootings within school grounds. Gun-free zones are magnets for deranged killers who hope to burn their names into the history books by running up big body counts. To such people, "gun-free zone" notices are open invitations to perpetrate their crimes unopposed. It is no mere coincidence that mass shootings repeatedly have occurred in designated gun-free zones.

What genius thought that a posted "gun-free zone" notice would be a deterrent? Does anyone believe that shooters would stop in their tracks out of fear of higher penalties for carrying guns into such areas? Would the risk of higher penalties have scared the many shooters who commit suicide at the scene?

Overwhelming evidence points to the single largest common factor in all of these incidents; most of the perpetrators were either actively taking powerful psychotropic drugs, or had been at some point not too long before they committed their crimes.

While evidence seems to be mounting that legal restrictions upon guns do not decrease overall crime rates, the fact remains that illegal firearms remain one of the biggest causes of crime in the country. In a world where law-abiding citizens do obey tough strictures on possessing firearms, illegal guns would seem to be even more dangerous as the only individuals to have guns in such a world would be those who do not obey the law.

Illegal guns clearly have an impact on the crime rate; they increase it to undesirable levels, while restrictions and laws on guns seem only to prevent citizens from having the necessary means to defend themselves.

> The start of a solution would appear to be a combination of actions. Combating illegal guns via greater police action, together with repealing some of the more restrictive gun laws, is a rational approach. This would free up resources to then aid in cracking down on illegal guns, as well as increasing the prevalence of legal guns which, as shown elsewhere, seems to have a negative effect upon crime rates. Thus, law enforcement systems could begin enforcing a policy concerning both legal and illegal firearms that would greatly decrease overall crime (The *Wall Street Journal*, September 25, 2014).

The most direct and simplest way to understand the political hyperbole behind the issue of gun control is to review a Q&A interview published by *Newsmax* (December 15, 2012) between David Patten and John R. Lott, one of the nation's leading gun experts, who is a college professor and author of *More Guns, Less Crime: Understanding Crime and Gun Control Laws* (in its third edition as of 2015):

Q: Dr. Lott, your work suggests people are more secure, rather than less so, when firearms are readily available in society.

A: Simply telling them to behave passively turns out to be pretty bad advice. By far the safest course of action for people to take, when they are confronting a criminal, is to have a gun. This is particularly true for the people in our society who are the most vulnerable.

Q: The media typically spins these mass shootings as an American phenomenon. They suggest we ought to be more like Europe, with strong gun control, because then we would not have these problems. Is that true?

A: No. Europe has a lot of multiple-victim shootings. If you look at a per capita rate, the rate of multiple-victim public shootings in Europe and the United States over the last 10 years have been fairly similar to each other. A couple of years ago you had a couple of big shootings in Finland. About two-and-a-half years ago you had a big shooting in the UK, 12 people were killed.

You had Norway last year [where 77 died]. Two years ago, you had the shooting in Austria at a Sikh Temple. There have been several multiple-victim public shootings in France over the last couple of years. Over the last decade, you've had a couple of big school shootings in Germany. Germany, in terms of modern incidents, has two of the four worst public-school shootings, and they have very strict gun-control laws.

The one common feature of all of those shootings in Europe is that they all take place in gun-free zones, in places where guns are supposed to be banned.

Q: Can you give readers an example of an incident where a teacher or authority-figure with a gun was able to thwart a violent shooting?

A: There was the university case in the Appalachian law school. You had the K through 12 in Mississippi and the one in Edinboro [Pennsylvania]. You had New Life Church [in December 2007]— you had 7,000 parishioners there when the person broke into the church with about a thousand rounds of ammunition.

But there was a woman there, a former Chicago police officer who had gotten a concealed handgun permit because she was being stalked by her ex-husband. She had asked permission from the minister there to be able to carry a concealed handgun. She was worried if she couldn't carry it at the church there that she would be vulnerable going to and from the church. She shot at him [the mass shooter] 10 times, wounding him, and he committed suicide. These types of cases occur all around us, and they usually don't get much attention, especially if they are stopped before people are injured or killed.

Q: How can society prevent such mass shootings, or are they avoidable at all?

A: About 75 percent of the time when these attacks occur, the killers themselves die at the scene. Even the times when they don't die, it seems pretty clear their intent was to die, but they just couldn't bring themselves to commit suicide, pull the trigger, and shoot themselves at the last moment.

But in their warped mind, what they want to do is commit suicide in a way that will get them attention, so people know who they were when they were here. It's a pretty sick idea, but if you read the documents that they leave, the diaries and the video tapes, it is pretty clear that these guys know that they get more attention the more people they can kill.

So their goal is to try to kill as many people as possible. So there are two issues here. One is focusing on the attention. And, I think it's pretty clear that if people stopped mentioning their names—I'm not saying that is possible—that's one thing that would reduce their incentive to go and commit these crimes.

The second thing is to give people the option to protect themselves. One of the things I've written about recently is the attack at the Aurora, Colorado movie theater. [In Aurora], you have seven movie theaters that were showing the *Batman* movie when it opened at the end of July, 2012.

Out of those seven movie theaters, only one movie theater was posted as banning permit-concealed handguns. The killer didn't go to the movie theater that was closest to his home. He didn't go to the movie theater that was the largest movie theater in Colorado, which was essentially the same distance from his apartment as the one he ended up going to. Instead, the one he picked was the only one of those movie theaters that banned people taking permit-concealed handguns into that theater.

The problem is, whether it is the earlier Portland [Oregon] shooting, or the Connecticut shooting [Newtown], or the Sikh temple attack in Wisconsin, time after time these attacks take place in the few areas within a state where permit-concealed handguns are banned. It's not just this year, it's all these years in the past. And at some point people have to recognize that despite the obvious desire to make places safe by banning guns, it unintentionally has the opposite effect.

When you ban guns, rather than making it safer for the victims, you unintentionally make it safer for the criminals, because they have less to worry about. If you had a violent criminal stalking you or your family, and was really seriously threatening you, would you feel safer putting a sign up in front of your home stating, "This home is a gun-free zone."

My guess is you wouldn't do that. And I've never run into any gun-control proponents who would do that either. And the reason is pretty clear: Putting a sign there saying this is a gun-free home isn't going to cause the criminals to say, "Oh, I don't want to break the law, so I'm not going to go in and attack these people." It encourages them to do it. It serves as a magnet for him, if he's going to engage in this attack, that that's the place where he is going to engage in, because he finds that it is going to be easier to do it there.

Yet every time we have one of these mass shooting incidents, it renews the call from the media and the left for banning guns.

I believe that the people who are pushing for these gun controls are well intentioned. I think they're wrong. I think the things they're going to make life more dangerous. But it's understandable. If you see something bad that happens, and it happens with a gun, the natural reaction is: "Well, if I take the gun away, bad things won't happen anymore." The problem is you have to realize that when you go and ban guns, you may only take them away from good law-abiding citizens and not the criminals. And to disarm law-abiding citizens just makes it easier for crime to occur, not harder.

You also have to think about self-defense. It is presumed that bad things happen with guns. But the news rarely covers people using guns defensively to stop crimes from happening. And that has a huge impact on people's perceptions about the costs and benefits of guns.

Q: So can you give us a correlation between crime rates in jurisdictions that try to ban concealed guns and the crime rate in those that do not?

A: If you look over past data, before everyone that was adopting [concealed carry laws], you find that for each additional state that adopted a right-to-carry law you'd see about a 1.5 percent drop in murder rates, and about 2 percent drop in rape and robbery. Just because states are right-to-carry doesn't mean they've issued the same number of fees. You have big differences in states' training requirements.

The bottom line seems to be when you make it costly for people to get permits, fewer people get permits. You particularly price out people who live in high-crime urban areas from being able to get permits, and those are the ones who benefit the most from having the option to defend themselves.

Q: Do gun-free zones invite these attacks?

A: Yes, they're magnets for these attacks. They make them more likely. These gun-free zones are really tiny areas within a state, and yet that's where these attacks occur time after time.

Whenever you see more than a few murders taking place, the odds are almost a hundred percent that they are going to occur at a place where permit-concealed handguns are banned. And they were doing it, ironically, in an attempt to try and make people safe. But the problem is it is law-abiding citizens who obey those bans, not the criminals.

Look at Virginia Tech, for example, where we had 32 people killed. If you were an adult with a concealed handgun permit, you could take your permit-concealed handgun virtually any place in the state, except for universities and a couple of other places. There are hardly any gun-free zones in Virginia. And yet, if you were a faculty member and you accidentally carried your permit-concealed handgun onto university-owned property there, and you got caught, you were going to get fired and your academic career would be over.

You're not going to get an academic job anyplace in the country. Same thing with the students: if you get expelled for a firearm-related violation, your academic career is over. Those are real penalties. Those people's lives are going to be dramatically changed. But if you take somebody who is a killer you would be facing 32 death penalties or 32 life sentences, plus other charges. And the notion that somehow the charge of expulsion from school would be the key penalty that would keep them from doing it, not 32 death penalties, is absurd. It just doesn't make any sense. It represents a much bigger real penalty for the law-abiding good citizens than it does for the criminals there.

So we have to think about who is going to be obeying these laws. And it's true for gun-control laws generally. One of the things I try and do in *More Guns, Less Crime* is show what happens to gun rates when guns are banned. It would be nice if things were that simple, that going and banning guns would eliminate crime.

But what you find happening is murder rates and violent crime rates go up. And the question is why. It's a pretty simple answer: because the law-abiding citizens are the ones who turn in their guns, and not the criminals.

Q: Would it be a good idea to have teachers who have concealed carry permits in the schools, to better protect kids?

A: I'm all for that. I've been a teacher most of my life. I've been an academic. I have kids in college still, and kids below that. It's not something that I take lightly. But it's hard to see what the argument would be against it.

People may not realize this, but we allowed permit-concealed handguns in schools prior to the ironically named Safe School Zone Act. And no one that I know has been able to point to a single bad thing that occurred, not one.

We changed the law, and we started having these public-school shootings. So I don't think they got the intended re-sult that they were hoping for with that type of ban. Right now, [some jurisdictions] allow you to carry concealed-permit guns in the schools. There are not a lot of them. But there are no problems that have occurred with any of those states, either.

Q: Could arming teachers and getting rid of gun-free zones have averted a tragedy such as we saw in Newtown, Connecticut?

A: Well, I think two things would happen. One is, we see the way these killers search out places where people can't defend themselves. So I think there's at least a very good chance that if it is known teachers and others there would have permit-concealed handguns, it would have dissuaded the attack from occurring to begin with. Secondly, even if he did attack, it would be by far the safest course of action.

The amount of time that elapses between when the attack starts and when someone can get to the scene with a gun is very important in determining the extent of the carnage. The faster you can get somebody [there], the more you can limit it. If you could get the police there in 8 minutes, which would be record time, that would be an eon for people who are there helplessly having to face the killer by themselves with no protection. (end of Q&A interview).

It appears that the priorities for human evolution favored intellectual growth followed by physical development. Left to "dry out" in last place is emotional progress. When left to fend for itself, uncontrolled emotion has the potential for deranged antisocial manifestations. Since progress in the emotional arena is not likely to take place in the short term, we must rely on society to develop means to cope.

CHAPTER 23

Political Correctness

• • •

What are the factors that predispose the concept of Political Correctness? Is Political Correctness related to the oxymoronically flavored concept of "moral equivalency" that world politicians employ when they apply selective standards of conduct that they find convenient to fall back upon when it serves their purpose?

Some background is necessary for this to be considered. Western civilization was founded on the Judeo-Christian concept that puts great emphasis on human uniqueness and the sacredness of each individual. No individual is to be determined to be inherently good or evil because of economic status, gender, ethnicity, sexual orientation, or race. Yet, depending on one's political orientation, these *groupings* of individuals are often deemed to be good or bad without consideration of their individuality. For example, a Communist believes that workers and the poor are good without any further consideration, and that entrepreneurs (the bosses) and the wealthy are bad. Communism goes further by characterizing the good as being victims of the bad. Behaving like a Communist undermines Western ideals and fosters a state of individual hopelessness by displacing the freedom of incentives.

In America, Political Correctness is a first step in constraining creative individualism by disallowing a recognition of our individuality. There are no longer any absolutes. "Bad" is excused and "good" is chastened, without individual consideration. As one example; the law breaking rioters in Fergusson Missouri, would have us believe that the man stealing from a fast food store is an innocent victim, and the subsequent police response was criminal. That is such a lop-sided and distorted judgement of the events that only a Politically Correct biased administration would conduct an inquisition after the considered decision of a grand jury.

These are not the hallmarks of the democracy that the United States has experienced for most of its history. Political correctness is the hallmark of a totalitarian regime. It is a political method of controlling by making equal.

> *Truth becomes something to be laid down by authority, which has to be believed in the interest of unity. It festers in an intellectual climate, which begets the loss of the meaning of truth and the disappearance of the spirit of independent inquiry. Differences of opinion in every branch of knowledge become political issues to be decided by authority. This can be found everywhere among intellectuals who have embraced a collectivist faith, and who are acclaimed as intellectual leaders even in countries still under a liberal regime. The end is the destruction of reason.*
> —Economist Friedrich Hayek, paraphrased
> from *The Road to Serfdom* (1944)

The progression of political correctness in a society cloaks the decline of democracy. The US Declaration of Independence, as we've discussed in earlier chapters, declares that "All men are created equal." Surely they are equal in rights and equal in opportunities without consideration of origin, but does that extend to meaning that, in a democratic society, "I am as good as you, in all aspects"? Is that the essence of Political Correctness? Is that what the heart of democracy believes?

This is how C. S. Lewis saw the issue of equality and might have viewed Political Correctness as it is treated in this chapter:

> For "democracy" or the "democratic spirit" (diabolical sense) leads to a nation without great men, a nation mainly of sub-literates, full of the cocksureness which flattery breeds on ignorance, and quick to snarl or whimper at the first sign of criticism. And that is what Hell wishes every democratic people to be...It would appear they're coming closer to getting their wish (*The Screwtape Letters*).

Political Correctness sacrifices free speech for correct speech, equality under the law for equalizing laws, truth for expediency, and justice for payback/revenge.

> *Excellence: can we be equal and excellent too?*
> —John W. Gardner, former US Secretary
> of Health, Education, and Welfare

Somehow, Political Correctness became an ideal in America for those who are blind to history and the current failed Socialist political experiments (the "Workers' Paradise," etc.). The most egregious expounders of this destructive concept are academic faculties that influence the gullible, wide-eyed young. Following closely behind is the media, which is an instrument of social control.

At the University of California at Irvine, the undergraduate legislative council passed a measure banning the American flag on campus. An online letter circulated with upward of twelve hundred signatures, including those of more than sixty UC professors who supported the ban-the-flag initiative. The letter stated that *"Nationalism, including US nationalism, contributes to racism and xenophobia."* Such sentiments represent a loss of love and respect for our country among some of America's youth and their educators. It is indicative of radical and misguided notions of the near-term and long-term history of America, a glaring dismissal of the heritage and traditions of our country, and the erosion of confidence in the exceptionalism that made the United States a model for the world. Such divisive and distorted concepts have their roots in Political Correctness.

Political Correctness also identifies minority groups that it characterizes as "marginalized." Then, in an identity-politics ploy, it endeavors to create a political mind-set that those "marginalized" are not part of the majority group, and that they can only become part of the majority through the constraint of others. Political Correctness is the opening shot for individualism to become a deviation. It is dangerous. It engenders fear. It is the political tool of those who would see the United States relapse into a conformist and controlled society. That is what predisposes the concept of Political Correctness. Political Correctness is the antithesis of innovation and mobility. It is a step backward for those who aspire for personal freedom.

When asked to define Political Correctness a former Commander-in-Chief mockingly replied, *Political correctness is a doctrine, recently fostered by a delusional, illogical minority and promoted by a sick mainstream media, which holds forth the proposition that it is entirely possible to pick up [a turd] by [the] clean end!* (Harry S. Truman, telegram to General Douglas MacArthur, September 1, 1945).

"Give 'em hell, Harry" didn't pull any punches. But nowadays, those who choose to rise above a politically correct mentality are labeled as racists or sexists or, failing that, simply characterized as being prejudiced (witness the roiling on college campuses against advocates of free speech). Aside from the Politically Correct issue, no one can deny that prejudice exists (see chapter 30). Prejudice, as a characterization, however, is misplaced when Politically Correct proponents choose to use it as a tool to obfuscate the truth.

CHAPTER 24

World Order

• • •

From time immemorial, people have formed societies whose bases consisted of tribes with like origins that were confined within natural geographic or self-defined boundaries. World War I changed that for much of Europe, for all of the Middle East, and for much of the rest of the world. Even before that cataclysmic event, the United States of America, being a nation of immigrants, was changing the ways that diverse peoples lived together.

Since World War II, we have witnessed the ever more forceful reformation of political boundaries. Vietnam, the Balkans, the Soviet Union, Israel, and much of the Arab Middle East reflect long-festering needs for human self-determination that will not be constrained by outside political manipulation and exploitation. Still festering are issues that involve the land and sea borders of China, Japan, the Philippines, Russia, Ukraine, Turkey, the Koreas, the middle East and others.

World order seems to be under attack. But first, what is world order? At different times and in different places, world order has been defined by colonialism, religious majorities, economic coercion, and the outcome of wars. Within each predominant world order was the snobbery that its proponents had the correct international prescription to forever settle the issue (Germany's Third Reich was to last for a "thousand years"):

* Colonialists kept order by the forceful suppression of indigenous peoples.

* Europe used power and statesmanship to constrain clashing national ambitions.

* The United States advocated the worldwide spread of democracy.

Americans applauded the American approach and took pride in the spread of democracy. We gave little consideration to acceptance from populations who do not hold with our concepts of free and representative governance, liberty, open markets, unlimited economic opportunities, and a melding of ethnic and religious precepts.

Underlying the American approach was the belief that we could simply and quickly enrich societies and bring world order by foisting our evolved sense of freedom and democratic governance upon the cultures of other sovereign states that have lived for eons with different values. While in some instances the American approach has worked, vast areas of the world never shared American values; some have only accepted them with reservations. Now that such reservations are surfacing, we have arrived at a turning point in our concept of world order.

Sovereign states evolved to be the formal units of international life, each having its own defined borders. Traditionally, world order was conditioned upon sovereign states weighing their national interests and accommodating a balanced equilibrium with other sovereign states. Europe diverged from that pattern by forming the European Union (EU). In doing so, the borders of its component states became "soft," but the bloc failed to develop a unity and cohesiveness of foreign policy (which was formerly reserved to each of its individual component nations). In other words, diminishing the authority of each member state created a wobbly coalition that is not truly unified in purpose and is hampered in its ability to respond to crises. The result is that the European Union has produced a power vacuum in its part of the world (and elsewhere) that fosters instability. A united Europe (EU) is not the same as our fifty states being united because the basis for the founding of the EU and the United States was very different (for the reasons cited above).

With borders melting away in the nearby Middle East and with the impunity of nearby Russia, the threat to the European Union is very real. Both world wars arose because neighbors appeared weak.

Asia is a different story. There is no power vacuum. On the contrary, in Asia any instability of world order is a product of disagreements between legitimate sovereign nations, with the potential to lead to serious confrontations.

Economic globalization ignores national borders and rides herd over the world. The foreign policies of sovereign powers have always reconciled themselves to these economic forces while, at the same, time serving their own national aims. This is not an easy balance, especially in democracies whose electorates vote to serve their own personal interests. An unstable world order, with the potential for confrontation, is the consequence of humans' inability to arrive at a selfless common purpose that could benefit all.

Excluding short-term dips, economic accommodation has produced unprecedented prosperity for those who worked within it, and with one another, for many decades. These are the winners of the world order. As one would expect, where there are winners there are losers. The losers (for instance, southern Europe) are the nations whose politics worked to negate or obstruct the system of the winners, and who are now undergoing a painful reevaluation, including the need for financial aid from the winners.

World order is contingent upon meaningful communications. Social-event summit meetings that end in pronouncements and joint declarations produce no changes of any substance. The reason is that such meetings do not result in common convictions that, more often than not, might be painful to some, or all, of its members. This issue goes directly to the premise of this book— the flawed evolution of humankind. Elected politicians are probably less capable of dealing with substantive issues than are many "lesser" folks.

> *I do not know if the people of the United States would vote for superior men if they ran for office, but there can be no doubt that such men do not run.*
>
> —Alexis de Tocqueville, *Democracy in America*

We are now undergoing a revision in world structure that will mark a sea change of great consequence. Regional spheres of influence are now emerging that may not be limited to currently existing sovereign states. As children are wont to do, these new spheres will be testing themselves against other spheres. In addition to swallowing large portions of geography (Crimea, South China Seas, the mid-East) any world order that emerges will have to contend with nuclear-armed spheres, with potentially devastating consequences.

To address and contain this new world, the United States must take the lead and do the following:

- Have strong politicians who will lead the rest of the world rather than pander to an electorate. No other nation will follow unless the United States is leading.

- Establish what actions it will engage in, with and without a coalition.

- Reward friends and allies (and no others).

- Be committed to go in at full strength (unlike the gradual escalation in Vietnam during the Johnson administration) and eliminate the sham of "rules of engagement".

- End Political Correctness and concerns of collateral damage. Civilian deaths are inevitable if the end game of war is winning. It is estimated that fifty percent of deaths in World War II were non-combatants. Without justifying collateral damage, it should be known that not all civilians are innocent.

- Develop a strong geopolitical strategy in order avoid starting anything without an end game. The motto of our Strategic air Command (SAC) was "Our Mission is Peace". They accomplished their mission by having nuclear armed B-52s bombers in the air at all times with preassigned targets. The USSR blinked and the Cold War ended.

We are at a pivotal point in history—more so than at any other time. Militarily and economically the United States dwarfs Russia, China,

Iran, and many other middle-Eastern areas. There is no guarantee that it will always be so. Carpe diem!

Especially alarming is that political leaders employ cover-up ruses to misdirect their personal agendas so as to foist a new world order in the mold of their "legacy". The most egregious example is the use climate control as a scare to remodel global economics (see chapter 19).

The real goal of climate control is *to change the economic development model that has been reigning for at least 150 years*, according to Christiana Figueres, a United Nations leader in forging a climate treaty. These fancy words simply mean that the United Nations endorses a redistribution of wealth among the nations.

CHAPTER 25

Health Care

• • •

"There's no such thing as a free lunch" is a popular aphorism that communicates the idea that it is impossible to get something for free.

> *I predict future happiness for Americans if they can prevent the government from wasting the labors of the people under the pretence of taking care of them.*
> —Thomas Jefferson

The search to provide universal health care has eluded a solution well into the twenty-first century. Again, evolved human nature is the key to understanding why the issues are so difficult to resolve.

Aside from the involvement of hospitals, the traditional players were the doctor and the patient. Sometime around the mid-twentieth century there entered a third party, the payer (generally in the form of an insurance company or government). Then the games began.

The players are as follows:

The Patient: Wants to be well and to have medical care with the least amount of out-of-pocket payments.

The Doctor: Wants to provide good care while earning as much as possible.

The Third-Party Payer: Wants to provide (insure) health-care benefits at the lowest cost possible.

That's a three-way conflict of interest with a myriad of potential outcomes. Here's where evolved human nature plays its role.

Let's take another look at those players again:

The Patient: Doesn't understand the complexities of health care and is uninterested in the cost so long as a third-party payer pays all.

The Doctor: Provides many tests to maintain his or her income (with constraints by the third-party payer).

The Third-Party Payer: Controls the other two parties by creating "participating doctors" systems to which patients are steered. Participating doctors agree to a reduced-fee schedule, but not to control the quantity of services rendered.

Question: What is the primary reason that health-care costs go up each year?

Answer: Consumers in a free competitive market provide the best guarantee of cost containment. Unfortunately, such is not the case for insured healthcare. Patients do not care about costs when they do not have to pay any out-of-pocket charges other than a small deductible.

Compounding patients' lack of interest in costs is our litigious society. Physicians minimize their malpractice risks by running all conceivable (often unnecessary) tests for a patient's condition, regardless of their costs, which, coincidentally, may also pad physicians' earnings. Who cares, so long as a third party is paying?!

Here's the solution to escalating medical costs:

A. Eliminate all up-front deductibles. Establish a selection of policies that have a fixed and fair fee allowance for each and every medical service (with no patient co-payment). If hospital or physician fees exceed the amount established, their patients will be on their own. In that way, patients will shop to keep their potential out-of-pocket costs within the proscribed reasonable and fair allowances.

That is the only way to keep a lid on rising costs.

As with every other consumer purchase, buyers (patients) must be part of the process; vendors (physician and hospital) must be required to be competitive. When this was tested in certain areas, some hospitals and physicians charged less than the proscribed allowances to attract patients, but never more. Here are a few more factors to consider:

- Cost will be predictable from year to year (fixed-fee allowances).
- Patients will not incur out-of-pocket charges (within the allowances) for care.
- Services, including excessive tests, will be reduced (see tort reform below).

B. The long-standing and traditional co-payment system was designed to be a cost-sharing process, but it turned out to be an abject failure. The reason is that physicians waived the co-payments so long as their fee allowances could be escalated quarterly (this comes from my own experience in the health-care insurance business). Without the necessity to pay a percentage of the fee (i.e., the co-payment), patients (buyers) are unconcerned about costs so long as they don't have to reach into their own pockets.

Without true-cost sharing, fees will always escalate, because no one is watching the store. And the consumer (patient) doesn't give a damn.

C. Institute tort reform: One feature of a new system should be that losers pay the winner's legal fees (as in the United Kingdom). Another consideration would limit the amount of contingency fee allowances so that plaintiffs would be required to pay a portion of the legal fees up front (there is a disincentive for plaintiffs to sue if there is a cost risk). Frivolous lawsuits would decrease as a result. The dockets would clear so much that it wouldn't take two to three years for cases to be heard. As it is now, too many lawyers are willing to risk only their time in the hope for a quick settlement.

Prior to federal-government health-care mandates, 14 percent of the US population had no health insurance (other than for the use of expensive emergency rooms). The rest were receiving the best health care in the world. Any logical thinker would not attempt to fix the part that "ain't broke" for most. Instead, a logical thinker would keep the majority as is and provide free health care for the "broken" 14 percent, even if it's totally paid for by taxpayers. The total cost to taxpayers for the 14 percent would be dramatically less than the cost of the government mandated system. Why downgrade the rest of society when the real and better solution for the 14 percent is obvious (and cheaper)?

If the federal mandates were good, the representatives who voted for the "plan" would be on the plan immediately.

The Congressional Budget Office (CBO) is Congress's fiscal scorekeeper and, as such, is widely respected by both Democrats and Republicans. The CBO is considered the gold standard of economic analysis. The CBO has reported that by 2024, the equivalent of 2.5 million American who were otherwise able and willing to work prior to the government's mandated health-care plan went into effect will work less, or not at all, as a result of that plan. This CBO conclusion has much to do with implicit marginal tax rates buried in the government's plan that will drive employment down.

Does that surprise anyone? Simply rephrased, if it were not for government intrusion into the health-care marketplace, 2.5

million more Americans would have full-time employment. Does the money-and-power trail enter into the government's motivation for the control of health care?

We should be open to anything that can improve society. Physicians take an oath to do no harm. That's where we should start. We should make no changes for the sake of change; if there are no current answers, we should wait. Bureaucracies, however, are run by humans whose self-perpetuation instinct necessitates that they justify their existence by creating changes, whether good or bad. Waiting is not in their cards. Waiting (doing nothing in the short term) is counterproductive to fulfilling their need for perpetuation; after all, pensions are at the end of their roads if they appear to justify their existence.

To really understand why federally mandated health care is not good, simply look at the Department of Veterans Affairs (VA). VA funding was $27.7 billion in 2003 and by 2013 had risen to $57.3 billion (a 106 percent increase). During that same time period the patient load had increased by a mere 30 percent. The VA is not short of money! What does the VA debacle tell us about federal mandates (and one payer systems)? Throwing money at a project frequently obfuscates an honest look at underlying mismanagement.

Paul Klugman is a *New York Times* columnist and economics professor at Princeton University (and a strong supporter of federal mandates). In 2011, Klugman praised the VA as a triumph of "socialized medicine." Yet, multiple audits beginning in 2009 made it clear that the VA was malfunctioning. It is this kind of socialist slanted reporting that tells us that federally mandated health care will reduce costs while providing access to health care (*you can keep your own doctor*). Keep in mind that a single payer system will perform like the VA. Fool me once, shame on you. Fool me twice, shame on me.

No Free Lunch

Anyone who has had to earn a living through the "sweat of his or her brow" knows that there is no free lunch. Folks who have inherited wealth may not understand that. Likewise, politicians behave as though there is no price to pay for giving out rewards ("free lunch") to those who vote to keep them in office.

It is often the case that payments come due after politicians leave office, and they leave with clean hands. But sometimes payments come due while they are still in office and at a time that they are seeking reelection. That is the time for us to hold their feet to the fire in the voting booth.

Government-sponsored health care is always touted as providing increased benefits with no increased costs (that free lunch again). That sounds like utopia but, for real life, it is all *Alice in Wonderland* stuff. Unfortunately, there is no realistic method to pay for those increases without printing more fiat paper dollars, raising taxes, or borrowing against our future.

Raising taxes is poisonous to voters. Absent a tax increase or borrowing, any increased costs must be passed on to consumers (patients). That is anathema to employee unions whose mandate it is to have employers bear the costs. Most employers have long-standing, multiyear contracts with unions that do not include the costs of increased benefits. The result: unions threaten to strike (thank you, federal government).

That provides a perfect opportunity (or excuse) for the government to issue edicts to mandate that employers foot the bill for these increased benefits. To employees and their unions, the government becomes a white knight charging to their rescue.

In that likely scenario, the additional costs for any new benefits will be passed on to consumers. That amounts to a hidden tax in which everyone will be paying, not just the people who get the higher benefits. Again, there's no free lunch.

Enrollment is one issue in the no-free-lunch scenario. The government touts that enrollment, if high enough to spread risk, will keep costs in check. "Enrollment figures" is a key issues that the government downplays.

To explain; imagine the cost escalation for any group when the costs of those who require medical care are not blended with the costs of those who require very little or no care. In insurance parlance this situation is called "adverse selection" and means that only those who require high pay-outs will be joining the plan (no spread of risk). Spreading the risk is only viable in controlling costs when *everyone*, regardless of individual health conditions, *must* become part of the insured group. It is human nature to avoid purchasing health insurance if there is little likelihood of needing care in the immediate future (this mainly applies to the young). Without the young who reqire minimal care, the risk is not spread. Costs skyrocket. Guess who pays?

To Illustrate: A senior citizen requires $9,000 per year of health care. A young person requires $1,000 per year. The administrator needs

$10,000 to pay the claims of both beneficiaries (the costs of administration not considered). The premiums paid for both are age dependent; the senior pays $7,000 annualy and the young person pays $3,000; total $10,000. Funding for all claims is covered. The senior is happy, he is getting more than he pays. The young person realizes that he is receiving less than he pays so he quits. Now, the adminstrator has only $7,000 in collected premiums from the senior to pay for $9,000 worth of claims. Again, guess who pays the difference?

The drafters of the federal health-care plan must have taken a cue from Abbott and Costello's "Who's on First?" routine:

1. In order to insure the uninsured, we first have to uninsure the insured.
2. Next, we require the newly uninsured to be reinsured.
3. To reinsure the newly uninsured, they are required to pay extra charges to be reinsured.
4. The extra charges are required so that those originally insured, who became uninsured and then became reinsured, are bearing enough extra costs so that the original uninsured can be insured, free of charge to them. Complicated? You bet!

Historical analysis of many countries demonstrates that one of the surest ways to promote the dependency of the populace on the government is to have the government control health care.

The money wasted to develop a system that nobody understands and is doomed to fail has already cost us billions and will continue to escalate. The ultimate cost will dwarf our expenditures for our military.

CHAPTER 26

Nutrition

. . .

So you think our medicine's pretty primitive? That's the wrong word. It isn't primitive. It's fifty percent terrific and fifty percent nonexistent. Marvelous antibiotics—but absolutely no methods of increasing resistance so that antibiotics won't be necessary. Fantastic operations—but when it comes to teaching people the way of going through life without having to be chopped up—absolutely nothing. Apart from sewage systems and synthetic vitamins, you don't seem to do anything at all about prevention. And yet, you have a proverb: prevention is better than cure.

—Aldous Huxley

"—medicine (is) *failed prevention—".*

Sir Michael Marmot, epidemiologist, *The Health Gap*

Whether or not you believe that the Bible is literal (creationism), or believe in natural selection (evolution), both point to a common source of human life. Does this mean that we are all the same in terms of our nutritional needs? No! Once migration took place, the multitude of varying environments, and what it took to survive local challenges, affected the evolved nutritional requirements of each group. This chapter is limited to only the foodstuffs to which humans had to adapt to survive in those varied environments.

Nutritional requirements are a function of evolution. The evolution of each surviving species of life on earth is linked to those foods that are associated with its distinct evolution, that is, their ancestral diet. Regardless of the rhetoric of the multitude of commercial products that appeal to the human desire to be thin or achieve health, few of those appeals address human existence in terms of who and what we evolved to be. There is a heavy price to pay for that oversight. Here are a few examples:

* Northern people (such as Scandinavians or Eskimos) and shore dwellers adapted to a diet heavy in fish.

* Inland peoples adapted to eating the meat of animals, grains, and fruit.

* Ice Age humans propagated by adaptation to eating the meat of animals that survived through their own adaptation of foraging through the permafrost for vegetation.

Today, through the gene adaptation of our migratory society, we have made slight accommodations to our obligation to adhere nutritionally to the evolved dietary requirements of our ancestors. Or at least it appears to be so. Findings from the Harvard School of Medicine posit that natural death should occur as a result of an almost simultaneous failure of our various organs within a short time of one another. That appears not to be the norm for our modern society. Instead, most natural deaths occur when one organ fails—heart, lungs, liver, pancreas, and so on. In other words, we are buried with many of our other organs perfectly healthy and functioning. If none of our organs failed prematurely (ahead of the other organs), the

Harvard thesis would play itself out and there would be no organ or tissue banks. There would be no need for them!

Why don't we, as complete organisms, survive to the total potential life-span of our colective organs? I suggest that most illnesses, including those that are terminal, are self-induced and brought on by our deviation from our evolved ancestral diet.

If, because of our natural ancestral evolution, what we ingest is difficult to metabolize, our endocrine systems (our systems of glands that produce hormones) will be stressed resulting in a hormonal inbalance. Unfortunately, this goes on, for the most part, without overt symptoms until an organ becomes so damaged that it manifests in some blatant clinical disorder or it becomes known as a result of a medical test. This book is not a medical journal reporting on the specifics of what might be an acceptable diet for humanitys'multitude of ancestral groups. There are certain foods, however, that are not acceptable for all groups, regardless of ancestral origin. This chapter will address just two of the most commonly ingested and harmful substances: sugar and caffeine.

Sugar is not a food; it acts like as drug, as does caffeine. Didn't you know that? Everone knows that sugar destroys teeth. Do you know, however, that after it destroys your teeth that it doesn't stop there? Do you believe that after you swallow sugar it becomes a healthful substance? Tooth decay is the first barometer of an unbalanced endocrine system and the first sign predicting future body breakdowns. Hormonal imbalance, even without clinical symptoms, will result in more serious illnesses later—sometimes many decades later.

Sugar and caffeine are both addictive drugs. Both create hormonal imbalances with unpleasant long term consequences. Sugar addiction reveals itself in cravings. Caffeine addiction manifests in an inability to start the day without a cup of coffee. Quitting either sugar or caffeine will induce withdrawal symptoms that are attributable to their addiction.

Sugar and caffeine are examples of substances that didn't make their appearances until very late in human evolution and, consequently, we have not adapted to them as foods. They create hormonal imbalances that result in long-term degeneration of our endocrine system. The results can be very nasty and surface as chronic and terminal illnesses resulting in premature death. Again, this book intentionally avoids providing detailed specifics of the effects of ingesting these harmful substances.

Associating an illness with old age may be a comfortable way of ignoring the discomforting thought that our lifestyles, especially our eating habits may, in fact, be suicidal. Equally as bad may be that we have blindly misplaced our trust in government-advisory bureaucracies who fail, for political or economic self-serving reasons, to serve us well. Why isn't sugar banned, or appropriately labeled, to protect an unsuspecting public? Follow the money trail.

Why do we have to eat at all? Eating is necessary to provide the raw materials to replace our body cells that are continuously dying. Some cells (skin) die by the minute. Other cells take years to die, but they all die. If that is the case, how do we as organisms survive? Answer: We replace those dying cells with new ones. Eating provides the source of the raw materials required to create new human tissue. Energy is simply a by-product of the process. Since human cells are primarily composed of protein, it is absolutely essential for a healthy survival that our diets contain sufficient quantities of protein that are suitable to replace the billions of cells that died.[27] Not being a diet advisory, this book will not detail the foods that are best suited to accomplish that task; however, readers are advised to keep in mind who and what we are relative to the ancestry of each of us.

---

27 Ingested protein is not in the form that comprises human tissue. It must first be broken down by our digestive process into amino acids that are the basic building blocks of protein, and then reconstructed into human protein. That breakdown process requires an acid environment. If the acids in our system are compromised by the aging process or diluted by liquid ingestion, insufficient new protein will be generated for our needs, resulting in long-term degradation of our tissues. Dilution occurs when liquids are taken with meals. Milk is especially harmful in that regard, because its high pH can nullify our normal digestive acids.

CHAPTER 27

Diet: Facts and Fiction

• • •

DISCLAIMER: Anything appearing in this book should not be construed as medical advice. That advice, for each person, should be limited to the purview of his or her physician.

POPULAR MYTHS

* The best way to lose weight is to reduce your fat intake.
* The best way to lower your cholesterol level is to reduce your fat intake.
* The best way to lower your risk of a heart attack is to lower your saturated fat intake.

The preceding three statements are all wrong, but they are such popular myths and accepted as facts that diet companies make fortunes promoting these fairy tales through their products. Further, the propagation of this mythology is often prescribed by physicians (who may caution against red meat, eggs, etc.).

In February, 2015, the Dietary Guidelines Advisory Committee declared certain fats and eggs are no longer the enemy and that cholesterol is "not considered a nutrient of concern for overconsumption." This after decades of advising Americans to "watch their cholesterol".

How did this all this misinformation come about?

Our distrust of saturated fat can be traced back to the 1950s to one man, Dr. Ancel Keys, who was known for developing the K-ration for use by the military in World War II. Keys was formidably persuasive and, through sheer force of will, he rose to the top of the nutrition world for relentlessly championing the idea that saturated fats raise cholesterol levels and, as a result, cause heart attacks.

A 2002 investigation of his research revealed that Keys violated several basic scientific norms in his study. For his investigation and to prove his preconceived thesis, Keys cherry-picked only those areas in which people had lived long on a diet that did not include meat and cheese. Keys excluded countries where various peoples had lived long lives on a diet of eggs and lots of fat.[28]

The 2002 investigation uncovered the bias in Keys's research technique but the misimpressions left by his erroneous data had already become international dogma. By 2002 the American Heart Association and the US Department of Agriculture had already

---

28 If Keys had selectively chosen to study Eskimos in the Arctic for his research, this is what he would have found: The normal diet of Eskimos contains an excessive amount of animal protein (280 g.) and much fat (135 g.). Interestingly, more than half of their low level of carbohydrates (54 g.) is derived as glycogen from the meat that is eaten. Eskimos have low rates of coronary-artery disease despite their high-fat and high-meat diet.

issued long-standing guidelines that made Keys's work the gold standard of a healthful diet.[29]

There was no turning back; a bias in favor of Keys's work had grown so strong that his conclusions just seemed like common sense.

What Keys overlooked was that primitive societies in the modern era who are insulated from the advance of Western influence suffer less from the degenerative pathologies that afflict modern humans: diabetes, cancer, cardiovascular disease and caries (tooth decay). The "primitives" enjoy better health without the availability of modern physicians and dentists.

Tooth decay, generally taken less seriously than other diseases, is mentioned here because of two issues: it is more prevalent than other pathologies, and it is the first indicator (in childhood) of an unbalanced body chemistry that will clinically manifest in more serious degenerative illnesses later in life. See chapter 26 for the culprits of modern diet.

While the world, including the medical community, was preaching the ills of meats, eggs, cholesterol, and fats, a few voices in the wind were investigating a different approach to understanding what constitutes a healthy diet for humans. It was the tried and true "learn from history" method that is characteristic of the discipline of anthropology. Anthropology pursued an investigation of

---

29 Proctor & Gamble raised $1.7 million (in 1948 dollars) to take the small American Heart Association to prominence. P&G makes Crisco (an oil hydrogenated into a solid) to use in lieu of butter and lard. In experiments on animals hydrogenated products lead to cirrhosis of the liver and early death, and are suspected of interfering with basic cellular functioning in humans. They have since been condemned by the Food and Drug Administration for their ability to raise our levels of LDL (bad) cholesterol.

the diet on which humankind survived and evolved (ancestral diet). Absent from our ancestral diet, for example, is vegetable oil for which there is no record of human consumption prior to 1900 (see below for more on vegetable oil). This is a short time in the grand scheme of evolution to expect our body chemistry to adapt to any marked deviation from the diet of our ancestors without a price to pay in illness and life.

In St. Pete Beach, Florida, Dr. Melvin Page, a dentist, built upon the works of Weston Price who first published *Nutrition and Physical Degeneration* in 1939. The book detailed a series of ethnographic nutritional studies that Price performed across diverse cultures. His research included the peoples in a remote area in Switzerland, Native Americans, Polynesians, Pygmies, and Aborigines, amongst many others.

Price claimed that various diseases that were endemic to Western society of the 1920s and 1930s were rarely present in non-Western cultures. He argued that as non-Western groups abandoned their indigenous diets and adopted Western patterns of living, they showed increases of typically modern Western diseases.

In his classic book *Degeneration Regeneration*, Page explores the underlying cause of why humans have such shorter life-spans than mammals that live in the wild (ten to fourteen times their puberty age). Ancient humans lived longer than we do today (excluding infant mortality and the imposition of modern medicine). After analyzing fifty thousand blood studies, human measurements, and the progression of modern degenerative diseases (heart disease, cancer, diabetes, etc.), Page commenced treating afflicted patients with a regimen of balancing their body chemistries through hormonal therapy and reversion to their ancestral diet, since it was their modern diet that unbalanced their body chemistry in the first place.

Modern culture has seen a number of Dr. Page wannabes who advocate dietary regimes that are similar, but not exactly the same, to his. One of the earliest and most recognizable members of this group was the late Dr. Robert Atkins. Many others have followed.

*F*AT

Modern humans' switch away from fats created a greater consumption of carbohydrates that not only exacerbated the problem of obesity, but accelerated the normal degeneration of our bodies.[30] Insulin is essential in metabolizing carbohydrates. Human insulin is produced by the pancreas. A healthy pancreas will produce insulin in a proportion necessary to deal with the quantity of carbohydrates that are ingested. In that process, high insulin levels will deposit fat, and low insulin levels will mobilize (burn off) fat. Ingesting fat in moderate quantities will not result in obesity. The culprit in obesity is carbohydrates.

That is exactly the premise of Page's work: an unbalanced chemistry will selectively degenerate one or several organs (the pancreas as in diabetes) and cause death, while all other organs remain apparently

---

30 The Harvard School of Public Health stated, "Medical treatment of older people also needs to change because the elderly contract multiple diseases, so curing one at a time does not extend life. We need to work on the commonality of diseases and find what is fundamental to squeeze the disease period to later in life."

healthy and functioning. Many healthy organs are buried with their dead host.

Death from Old Age

Many Jews (and perhaps others) recite a blessing in which they bestow: "You should live to be 120." Where did this tradition come from? Is there any basis for it?

Based on the life-span of mammals in the wild, 120 years is about ten to fourteen times their puberty age (see above). That life-span may actually be correct if we live to old age and not die from the failure of one or more organs while the remaining organs are still healthy. That is the message of the Harvard study (footnote 30). Death from old age should come when all organs stop working within a short period of time of one another as a result of being "worn out," not because of disease. And the natural occurrence of that may be at about 120 years of age. These data and conclusions are drawn from the research of Melvin Page.

Meat Eaters

On the subject of carnivores, perhaps the commentary shown below says it best:

> Steven Shapin, in his review of Tristram Stuart's *The Bloodless Revolution*, extensively examines the medical, philosophical, and religious reasons for and against a vegetarian diet. But there is also an evolutionary argument for humans to consume meat.

While one can now thrive on a carefully considered purely vegetarian diet, for the past two million years hominids have evolved a digestive system meant for an omnivorous diet high in meat protein. Meat is far more readily digested by humans than fibrous and cellulose-rich plants and our ancestors benefited from its nutritional advantages, including the documented rapid growth of brain tissue—a development that was necessary for the very ideas of philosophy and religion that Stuart emphasizes as the vegetarians' rationale for the rejection of meat. This is to say nothing of the advantages that meat has given us in the form of healthier pregnancies, better breast-feeding, and longer life expectancy. Vegetarianism is fine, if done properly; but from an evolutionary perspective the arguments regarding the morality of eating animals fall quickly by the wayside, unless one would prefer to be the eaten rather than the eater (Christopher Kovats-Bernat, assistant professor of Anthropology, Muhlenberg College, letter to the editor, *New Yorker*, February, 2007)

Finally, wealthy countries suffer an epidemic of obesity that, aside from ingesting an unhealthful diet, comes from simply overeating. Why do people overeat? A partial answer is that it is a function of socializing. A more complete answer lies in the fact that the good taste of food is gratifying and satisfies certain hedonistic desires. Why has it not become widely practiced and socially acceptable to simply chew food for its gratifying taste and then spit it out? The answer lies with our evolution; the taste buds with the most pleasurable sensation are located so far back on our tongues that it is almost impossible to get that pleasure without swallowing. As an experiment, try to move food far back on your tongue without swallowing. Notice the heightened pleasurable taste that exceeds the taste enjoyment of simply chewing. Forced swallowing is a survival mechanism!

CHAPTER 28

Fluoridation by Government Mandate

• • •

Many municipal governments have mandated the fluoridation of their community water supplies. Consequently, young and old in those communities will be ingesting a known and cumulative poison. Fluoride is classified as a toxin and endocrine disruptor, and has never been approved as a drug by the Federal Drug Administration (FDA).

This is another example of big-government control. Where do you stand on the issue of governmental control versus individual liberty (see chapter 15 for choices)?

I was a practicing dentist for forty-nine years and have more than a passing acquaintance with the issues of fluoride in community water supplies. Certainly, government should have a role in mandating certain preventive health measures (e.g., vaccinations) for contagious diseases if there are no long-term adverse effects. But fluoridating the water of an unsuspecting populace is not one of them. In fact, a number of countries have banned it.

Vaccination is the wonder tool that it is because it is a biologic technique to stimulate our own defense mechanism against pathogens. And, any given vaccination is, for the most part, very infrequently repeated. This is not the case with the repeated and cumulative effect of the everyday ingestion of fluoridated drinking water from a tap.

Fluorine is a naturally occurring chemical; it is one of the halogen elements, all of which are toxic to human beings. It was accidently discovered during the first decade of the twentieth century that people who lived in communities whose water supply naturally contained fluoride had fewer incidents of dental caries (i.e., cavities). It was also noted, however, that many of those residents suffered from fluorosis (chalky white spots on the teeth).[31] Dental fluorosis is the visible sign of systemic toxicity that results in skeletal fluorosis and the potential ailments of arthritis, fibromyalgia, thyroid disease, and Alzheimer's disease. A 1992 study by the New Jersey Department of Health found higher rates of osteosarcoma (bone cancer) in adolescent males drinking fluoridated water when compared to non-fluoridated water.

Are fewer cavities a good exchange for introducing a known toxin into our bodies? Public-health leaders have maintained that low doses of fluoride are safe. Are those studies flawed (or worse, politically motivated)?

---

31 The first evidence of excessive fluoride exposure is whitish flecks or spots, particularly on the front teeth. Less known to the public is that fluoride also accumulates in bones. "The teeth are windows to what's happening in the bones," explains Paul Connett, professor of chemistry at St. Lawrence University in New York. In recent years, pediatric bone specialists have expressed alarm about an increase in stress fractures among young people in the United States. Connett and other scientists are concerned that fluoride— linked to bone damage by studies since the 1930s—may be a contributing factor.

"Information was buried," concluded Dr. Phyllis Mullenix, former head of toxicology at Forsyth Dental Center in Boston, and now a critic of fluoridation. Animal studies conducted by Mullenix and coworkers at Forsyth in the early 1990s indicated that fluoride was a powerful central-nervous-system (CNS) toxin, and might adversely affect brain functioning, even at low doses. (New epidemiological evidence from China adds support, showing a correlation between low-dose fluoride exposure and diminished IQ in children.) Mullenix's results were published in 1995, in a reputable peer-reviewed scientific journal.

During her investigation, Mullenix was astonished to discover there had been virtually no previous US studies of fluoride's effects on the human brain. Then, her application for a grant to continue her CNS research was turned down by the US National Institutes of Health (NIH), where an NIH panel, she says, flatly told her that "fluoride does not have central nervous system effects." Is that so? Is that another Big Brother power play?

Recent announcements by Harvard scientists show an average 7 to 14 percent deficit in IQ testing among adolescents living in fluoridated areas. Harvard also disclosed that males under twenty years of age have exhibited a sixfold increase in bone cancer in fluoridated areas (see 1992 New Jersey study above). Harvard also linked ADD, autism, and cognitive delays to the fluoridation of municipal water.

All long-term government studies on the potentially deleterious effect of fluoride are flawed because we do not have, as yet, sufficiently sophisticated tools to distinguish and separate the insidious etiology of long-term, premature degeneration in an aged population. Following are some other examples of our learning the hard way:

- Lead and asbestos were part of our homes and environment for a very long time before statistical evidence incriminated them (asbestos is a naturally occurring mineral).

- The Red Cross contributed to the popularity of cigarettes by freely distributing them to US doughboys in World War I. As late as the 1960s, the film industry depicted our screen heroes as sophisticates who smoked. Doctors endorsed cigarettes on TV. Those, and many other substances that subtly and insidiously poisoned our bodies ultimately created epidemics of diseases for which individuals and society are now paying a heavy price.

- For more than twenty years, physicians prescribed estrogen-replacement therapy for postmenopausal women until it was observed that those women were developing breast cancer.

Why did we not question the long-term and ultimate effect of these deadly things sooner? Is it possible that as fragile human beings we have a need to believe that government knows what is best for us?

In order to reduce dental decay all we have to do is reduce sugar (as we did with asbestos and lead). So, why does our government keep promoting public-water fluoridation? Perhaps it ignores the issue because there is no current medical way to grasp the long-term (i.e., lifetime) effects of fluoride. The effects are insidious and, at present, not measurable. How can anyone know if a life is shortened by ten years, or if the body's resistance to cancer or cardiovascular diseases is reduced by a chronic buildup of a toxin (fluoride)? Still, have physicians all forgotten their obligation to do no harm?

More likely the medical and dental communities, as well as the government, are reluctant to take on the well-funded and established sugar industry and to acknowledge that they have misdirected the public by promoting such an unknown and potentially deadly substance as fluoride.

For those who still believe that the benefit of fluoride outweighs the risk, there is always the route of prescription fluoride or fluoride added to bottled water. Government should not mandate the addition of any substance to public waters until such time as medicine can, without equivocation, run reliable, lifetime-length, double-blind studies for large certifiably similar groups of people.

CHAPTER 29

Curiosity

• • •

The definition of "curiosity" is the desire or eagerness to know about something or to get information.

Curiosity drives many forms of life. It is a force, derivative of evolution, that enables life to sustain itself, advance itself, or die in the process. It is the force behind not only personal human development but developments in other facets of human involvement such as science, language and industry.

Curiosity is shared at all ages, from birth to death. It manifests as a motivated desire for awareness that stems from a passion for information and knowledge. Even without being aware of a desire for knowledge, toddlers will crawl about until they find something of interest.

Humans differ from animals in the way in which their curiosities express themselves. While animals do have an innate exploratory nature, the desire for knowledge is unique to humans. Animal curiosity may have rewards, such as detecting food or, in the case of domestic pets, receiving affection from their masters. Human curiosity can be rewarded with new information and knowledge that, apart from having intrinsic value in itself, has the potential to reduce the undesirable state of uncertainty.

Humans are driven by many emotions (see chapter 7). Uncertainty is one of the most disturbing of emotions and has a compelling negative impact on the "peace of mind" that so many of us seek. That can be fertile ground for the search and exploratory elements of curiosity to manifest. Even those of us who benefit from having peace of mind may be compelled to seek issues to explore. That is where individual human genetics may come into play in terms of reaching for rewards beyond peace of mind. In that regard, new brain research is exploring the role of neurotransmitters such as dopamine, serotonin, cortisol, and opioid chemicals. That is beyond the scope of this book to investigate, however, and beyond my level of expertise.

With no intention of being flip, the following applies to people who act or speculate beyond their knowledge and level of expertise: "Curiosity killed the cat." This is a metaphor used to warn of the dangers of unnecessary investigation or experimentation. Any benefits that might accrue from curiosity requires an attention span that is sufficient to process information and apply that information. That also is a function of brain genetics.

All of the above notwithstanding, memory is the final link. Without the capability of recall, everything that we have previously explored and learned must be relearned in an endless cycle: recall the movie *Groundhog Day* (also see chapter 33).

Inciting curiosity requires a stimulus whether overt or subconscious. What motivates us individually?

- Is it an altruistic drive to help others? Can we produce a new medicine? There's nothing to lose by trying (except money, time and effort).

- Is it a search for a higher meaning to life (see chapter 9)?

- Is it a desire for social justice and peace? Should we engage in war to restore harmony among nations (chapter 4)? There's nothing to lose except life and culture!

- Is it a desire to accumulate money (see chapter 11)?

- Is it a desire for power (see chapter 16)?

Curiosity evolves. As one door opens, more doors appear that had gone unnoticed (and not necessarily to the same investigator). Curiosity is the father of knowledge (see chapter 1).

CHAPTER 30

Racism/Prejudice

• • •

Some are to blame, all are responsible.
—Rabbi Abraham Joshua Heschel

Discrimination against *the other* stems from fear (see below) and takes the form of sexism, religious intolerance, homophobia, age bias, racism and other manifestations. Racism is one of the more transparent prejudices in American society and, although showing progress, is not limited to targeting the African-American segment. All races are potential targets of other races.

Racism is so ingrained that it has been known to surface even among interracial married couples. I had a very close male acquaintance who was in a mixed race marriage. Despite the fact that his wife loved and married him (and had his children), she was not accepted by his parents. Even he (the husband) accused his wife, —*his own wife*—of being a racist. That demonstrates how ingrained is racism!

Because of humanities' evolved knowledge of self (see chapter 5) we retain an internal struggle between the good of tolerance and the bad of any form of prejudice. Consequently, everyone—*everyone*—is more or less prejudiced to some degree

Racism is one form of prejudice. Other forms of prejudice include nationalism, religious exclusivism, and gender bias. Prejudice even extends to age differences within the same group. Most forms of prejudice stem from an inherent need for immortality that takes the form of believing that you're better than those who are not like you (the biblical "other").

In extreme forms, prejudice would have groups killing other groups (the "other") to gain favor in the eyes of their God. If you're chosen (as most groups believe that they are), it follows that the "other" must not be favored by God and, therefore, you are doing God's work in killing them off: witness the Spanish Inquisition, the Turkish genocide of Armenians, Nazi Germany's Holocaust, South African apartheid, the Khmer Rouge in Cambodia, the ongoing wars between Shiites and Sunnis, and too many others to list.

The response of bystanders to those who hate the "other" may be what determines how much the haters can get away with and whom they target after they are done with hating their current "other."

> *The opposite of good is not evil, it is indifference.*
> —Rabbi Abraham Joshua Heschel

The Talmud, an early interpretive collection of Jewish law, teaches that your thoughts and motivations are of little consequence; what matters are your deeds. And those deeds are a measure of your being just.

Even if you are not religiously inclined, justice is measured by what you do, not by what you think or what your motivations are.

Here are a few examples:

* Lyndon Johnson was bigoted against Blacks, but he attempted to further Black causes.

* Richard Nixon was bigoted against Jews, but he took a great risk to save Israel.

RACISM IN AMERICA

In 1964, the Civil Rights Act became the legal response to American racism. The Act addressed prejudices based upon color, religion, gender, race, and national origin. Foremost in the charge to attack the sins of prejudice were Blacks (supported by certain religious groups). It was a movement of great moral clarity, championed by Martin Luther King Jr. and others.

During the succeeding decades the movement, as envisioned by King, has lost its focus, not because it was wrong but because it was successful. The America that existed in 1964 is not, for the most part, the America of today. The year 1964 could not have seen Blacks in the offices of president and attorney general and holding a considerable number of seats in Congress; Blacks in 1964 would not have held local political offices or headed corporations.

The Census Bureau reported in 2013 that Black-voter turnout was the highest for any racial group in the United States, "the result of a steady increase in Black voting rates since 1996." Overall, Black turnout accounted for a higher share of the vote in 2014 than it had in 2010.

Does anyone still believe that racism and the legacy of slavery are greater today than in past decades?

> *It's not a question of the disproportion between blacks and whites, or Asians, but the disproportion between blacks of today and blacks of the previous generation, and that's what's scary. I distinguish what might be between the legacy of slavery* [when Black communities were safer] *and what's the legacy of the welfare state where there is a palpable retrogression—the key one is the growth of the single-parent family.*
> *For every year from 1994 to the present, black married couples have had a poverty rate in single digits. Those people who have not followed the culture—the ghetto culture—are doing fine.*
> —Thomas Sowell, economist

So, where does the civil-rights movement stand today? Does it have any leaders of the stature of King or the correctly righteous heroism of Rosa Parks? What principles does it espouse today? Does it have any relevance?

There are reasons to continue challenging the ills of racism. The self-proclaimed civil-rights leaders of today, however, have misdirected their efforts toward self-aggrandizement rather than focusing on the issues of relevance for today's Black communities. Their moral authority is dead, and they embarrass themselves by having no other outlet than for causes, riots, and parades that are irrelevant to basic racist issues.

White effrontery against Blacks, although it still exists, is at a low level. Yet today's best-known civil-rights leaders still use that issue as their cause célèbre to justify their continuation in the limelight. Money and power derived from the gullible masses whom the leaders describe as "victimized" are what matter to these leaders.

Unfortunately, certain high-ranking Black politicians and their race-baiting cronies "do all they can to feed the sense of grievance, victimhood, and resentment because that's where the votes are," according to Sowell, in his 2015 book, *Wealth, Poverty and Politics: An International Perspective.*

Federal bureaucracies have a vested interest in fomenting and perpetuating racial divisiveness. Once an organization such as the Equal Opportunity Commissions (EEOC) is created to find discrimination, no one should be surprised when it finds discrimination lurking where no one thought to look.

Commendably, there are certain Black spokespeople (Dr. Ben Carson and Thomas Sowell, among others) who have bravely risen to identify and articulate the reasons why many Blacks remain economically challenged and why they fill American jailhouses. Throwing federal money at their problems is never an answer. Government is not the answer; it is the problem.[32] For further explanation, see chapter 15.

---

32 The net effect of preferential treatment (affirmative action, etc.), which is preferential more in intention than in results, is that those Blacks who are particularly disadvantaged have fallen farther behind under these policies. For example, Blacks who have relatively less work experience, lower levels of education, or female-headed families have all fallen further behind during the more than a decade of affirmative action. Black female-headed families have had an absolute decline in real income over this span (Thomas Sowell, 1983).

The difficulties that are experienced by the poor segment of Black America are a result of liberal welfare programs. Those government programs fostered enmity toward traditional morality and decimated Black families.

In the same year that saw the Civil Rights Act, Daniel Patrick Moynihan, assistant secretary in the Department of Labor under Lyndon Johnson, issued a report that stated, "the evidence—not final, but powerfully persuasive—is that the Negro family in the urban ghettos is crumbling." Marriage was discouraged through the subsidization of single parents. The government paid mothers to keep fathers out of the home—and paid them well. At the time of the Civil Rights Act, 25 percent of Black children lived in households headed by a single mother. Fifty years after the Civil Rights Act more than 70 percent of all Black births were to unmarried women (as compared to 35 percent for White births). How much of teen pregnancy, drug abuse, and dropping out of school is attributable to the increase in the numbers of absentee fathers that was fostered by government intrusion?

Racial paternalism, and its unintended consequences, can be as poisonous and pernicious as any other form of discrimination. The Constitution bans discrimination by those who wish to oppress a race or by those who have a sincere desire to help.
—Justice Clarence Thomas (*Adarand Constructors v. Pena*, 1995)

Our Constitution is color-blind, and neither knows nor tolerates classes among citizens.
—Justice John Marshall Harlan (in his
dissent of *Plessy v. Ferguson*, 1896)

[That] the *Constitution is colorblind is our dedicated belief.*
—Justice Thurgood Marshall (*Brown v. Board of Education*, 1954)

In view of the preceding opinions from justices of our Supreme Court, how did affirmative action play out in terms of its impact on the nation and, specifically, the Black population of America?

The proponents of affirmative action make a compelling argument for supporting educational benefits that would create a diverse student body. On the other hand, the long-standing demand of the civil-rights movement for equal treatment under the law would appear to conflict with any argument supporting affirmative action which is, in fact, de facto discrimination.

In 2006, the state of Michigan adopted an amendment to its constitution that addressed this conflict-of-principle issue by affirming the "equal rights under the law" principle. In Michigan, preferences in public education, public employment, and government contracting are now unlawful. The debate will continue.

Suffice it to say for this chapter that education and the return to nuclear families, together with the resurfacing of new and respected leaders, are the prerequisites to societal advancement. Progress for minorities means progress for America. Progress is best served through the creation of businesses and jobs. Progress cannot happen when riots destroy communities and businesses.

Finally, is it hypocritical to speak of a human race in a society that divides its members by race? Can humankind accept that there is a possibility that everyone's ancestors were of one race? Can science support such an assertion? What do theologians believe to have been the skin color of Adam and Eve?

The relatively recent discoveries of DNA researchers on the bones of ancient humans are instructive:

> "Two genes that effect skin color were also subject to rapid evolutionary selection as early farmers tried to subsist on grain-rich, vitamin-D-poor diets in northern areas with low levels of sunlight (sunlight helps the body to convert a form of cholesterol into a form of vitamin D). The shift to pale skin (which produces vitamin D more efficiently than darker skin) among northern Europeans, after the advent of farming, appears to have proceeded rapidly, pointing to some of the strongest selection pressures ever recorded in human genetics."
> —The *Wall Street Journal*, May 2, 2015

So what had been the skin color of the folks who mutated to a lighter skin to survive in the lower-sunlight environment of northern Europe?

CHAPTER 31

Language

. . .

East is East and West is West, and never the twain shall meet.
—Rudyard Kipling

About six to seven thousand languages are spoken today. Although lower forms of life have the ability to communicate, none of their systems matches the complexities of human language. The study of languages (or, more properly, linguistics) is far too complex to be properly addressed in this book whose thesis is evolution. Interested readers are encouraged to research this subject on their own.

Language is a communication tool through which representations in the human mind can be transmitted to another. Consequently, language is acquired through social interaction. In other words, words are created through social interaction and have meaning only within the context of peoples speaking the same language.

The myriad of languages spoken on this planet came about to serve evolving communicative and social needs within distinct human groupings and, therefore, is deeply entrenched in the culture of the group. The formative processes that resulted in languages were complex and varied. As a result, the words that form one language can only be translated into another language at the risk of miscommunication. As simple a proclamation as the English language "I love you" when translated into the German *Ich liebe dich* may not capture the emotions inherent in one to the other. Imagine what is lost in more complex business and political translations! Why are there such differences?

Environment, climate, geography, and all other such variables that had an impact on the ways that human races evolved also affected the cultures that formed the languages that evolved with them.

Syntax principles govern how words are combined to form phrases and utterances to establish the sentence structure for any individual language. For example, the syntactical rules of a language determine why a sentence in English such as "I love you" is meaningful, but "Love you I" is not.

Language is a product of (and is deeply entrenched in) culture. People think in their developed tongues, that is, language shapes their thoughts. Therefore, when different people are confronted with the same scenarios their thoughts will differ from one person to another because their thoughts are constructs of their cultures and native languages. As an example, whatever a word may mean to one group of people may have developed other nuances if it appears in another language. For example, *latte* may mean one thing to a New York Starbucks patron while having quite different meaning to someone in an Italian ristorante. Hence, there is an inbuilt potential for misunderstanding and conflict when translating from one language to another.

Spoken words and utterances are just one of hundreds of ways in which humans and other animals communicate. Experienced translators consider voice tones, body language and other signs that are inherent in verbal communications but are not conveyed in written communications.

CHAPTER 32

Immigration

• • •

Nations other than the United States have historically made the issue that they have evolved racially pure, i.e., pure Japanese as an example. Native Americans notwithstanding, the United States has always prided itself as being a nation of immigrants. The combining and survival of folks from so many various sources has produced a society that has blended evolutions into a mix of the best of what was brought to our shores, resulting in an exceptionalist, can-do culture.

> *"Keep ancient lands, your storied pomp!" cries she / with silent lips. "Give me your tired, your poor, / Your huddled masses yearning to breathe free, / The wretched refuse of your teeming shore. / Send these, the homeless, tempest-tost to me, / I lift my lamp beside the golden door!"*
> —Emma Lazarus, *The New Colossus*

The Irish potato blight that started in 1845, and the ongoing British suppression, prompted the start of a mass emigration from all of Europe lasting to the start of World War I. The result created a sea change in the character of American society. A common thread running through those émigrés during that period of time was the desire to assimilate and become Americans. By the next generation, the children of early immigrants had begun to discard their native tongues.

Toward the latter half of the twentieth century, the White emigration from Europe was supplanted by non-White émigrés from Asia, Latin America, the Middle East, and other non-European countries. The character of that new immigration differed from before, in that some of the newcomers were not motivated to assimilate. Pride and multiculturalism have become the divisive mantra of the Left (see chapter 23 on Political Correctness). Jeff Jacoby (*Boston Globe*) echoes this sentiment:

> *Americans thought it only natural that immigrants should strive to become American, and immigrants of all backgrounds could feel that they were part of a single national family. The rise of militant multiculturalism undermined this consensus. Today's "progressives" tend to regard the old ideal of patriotic assimilation as a form of cultural suppression. Instead of celebrating a common American culture, they pursue "diversity," and elevate racial, sexual, and ethnic identities over national identity. E pluribus unum has been turned on its head.*

Some émigré groups have asserted that American law is not applicable to them. They cling to the laws and courts that they brought with them, Sharia law being one example. Others, within their own communities, trade in the currencies of their original homelands. For example, Brighton Beach, New York, was a mecca for Russian émigrés several years ago. I recall shopping in that community during the early stages of their settlement. The prices on items for sale was displayed in rubles.

The immigrant is not Americanized unless his interests and affections have become deeply rooted here…until he comes to possess the national consciousness of an American.
—Supreme Court Justice Louis Brandeis

In 1819, John Quincy Adams wrote the following to a German citizen who was considering a move to America: [Immigrants] *must cast off their* [foreign] *skin, never to resume it. They must look forward to their posterity, rather than backward to their ancestors.*

What distinguishes the old from the new immigration to America?

- The old made a clean break from their ancestral homelands to seek new lives for their families. They fully accepted that they might never again see those whom they left behind.

- Many, though not all, of the new émigrés have come to America for employment opportunities and higher wages with the expectation of someday returning to their homelands. Witness the reverse migration when American jobs become scarce. Such reverse migration has become a grave situation in the border state of Sonora, Mexico, for example, which is unable to handle the influx of those returning to Mexico.

I posit that one obstacle to assimilation are the numbers of émigrés within any particular ethnic group that achieve a critical-mass status. Their "strength in numbers" enables them to form and retain their own unassimilated communities within the United States. Illegal status is another, perhaps more formidable, obstacle. Both issues are legal and societal issues that need to be addressed to sustain Emma Lazarus's vision of America as "The New Colossus."

CHAPTER 33

Memory

• • •

If I knew things would no longer be, I would have tried to remember better.

—Sam Krichinsky (played by Armin Mueller-Stahl) in the 1990 movie *Avalon*.

Certain failures of memory, coupled with human emotions, are intimately linked to individual and global history (see chapter 3). The failure to apply lessons that should be associated with memory is a glaring result of genetic discounting of the blessing and curse associated with such failure.

It is commonly said that a woman would not have more than one child if she remembered the pain of childbirth.

> *Unto the woman* [God] *said: I will multiply thy pain and thy travail; in pain thou shalt bring forth children.* (Genesis 3:16)

So, memory failure, especially in its details, can be a blessing, especially with the loss of a loved one.

The wounds remain. In time, the mind, protecting its sanity, covers them with scar tissue and the pain lessens. But it is never gone.
—Rose Kennedy

Shorter-term personal events are less likely to be remembered than longer-term personal events.

Ask a physician to recount Fleming's discovery of penicillin (in 1928) as he or she learned the story as a young medical student. Then, ask the same physician to recite the names of the last five patients for whom he or she prescribed the antibiotic.

Historical remembrance is a blessing that affords humankind the building blocks to learn and progress. That appears to be true in science, medicine, and other measurable progressions.

The curse is that historical remembrance, by way of a cause-and-effect learning tool for progress, is rarely applied to societal interchanges.

Wars, politics, laws, and so on, are reflective of not taking lessons from history about what is beneficial and what is detrimental to humankind's social progress. Emotions may be the barrier that stand in the way of progress (see chapter 4).

When the past no longer illuminates the future, the spirit walks in darkness.
—Alexis de Tocqueville

Long and Short Term Memory

For the purposes of this article, organic (automatic) memory will not be considered; an example of this type of memory is that the heart doesn't forget to beat.

Biologically speaking, the human brain functions differently with respect to long-term and short-term memory.

An astronomically large number of brain cells are required simply to generate consciousness. As a result, the human brain is limited in its ability to create and retain complex moving imagery. The limitation of that capacity has an impact on both long-term and short-term memory.

Short-term memory is the ready state of the conscious brain to absorb current and recalled scenarios. It can scan about seven words or symbols in about one second. Then, within thirty seconds, it forgets most of that information.

Long-term memory, not being conscious, has an almost unlimited storage capacity in the brain and much of it is retained for life. It takes repetition over a longer period of time, however, for long-term memory to develop. Long-term memory warehouses specific events and recalls them in a time sequence, that is, according to what happened first, then to what happened last. Long-term memory also links those events to consequences, that is, our long-term memory links fire to the suffering of burns. Those linkages are retained learning mechanisms that we use for future recall. It is the linkage that provides meaning to event recollection.

The recall of images with no links is simply *memory*. In contast, the recall of images *with* links is *remembrance*, especially if it is affected by the brain's emotional circuits. The conscious mind has the ability to recall what is stored in long-term memory and connect it with current scenarios; it can then hold both long-term and current scenarios in our short-term memory for brief intervals.

Memory is the blessing that we disparage by failing to learn from humanity's historical failures. And yet we make pronouncements such as "The War to End All Wars," "Never Again," and so on—at least until the next time. Our need to constantly reinvent the wheel is a plague visited upon humanity because we lack the emotional ability to divest ourselves of ego. Divesting ourselves of ego would compel the honesty of acknowledging that there is nothing new under the sun (see preface).

The Talmud asserts that God created repentance before creating the universe. Whether one believes in God or not, it's a compelling concept. It emphasizes that we are fated to misstep, but also have the capacity to undo some or all of the harm we cause. But as the thinking goes, God only provided us with this tool: it is up to us to use it.

CHAPTER 34

Extinction

• • •

For believers, God created humans on the seventh day of Creation. Somewhere along the way God also created the means for humans to become extinct. Notwithstanding the Four Horsemen of the Apocalypse (as described in the Book of Revelation), the top pathways to the end of humankind include wars, collisions with comets or asteroids, and epidemics (not in that priority).

Wars, throughout the ages, have taken a huge toll of human lives. The human toll from World War I was thirty-seven million lives; for World War II it was sixty million lives (2.5 percent of the world's population at the time). In any future war, which will likely include the use of weapons of mass destruction (WMDs), the death toll will most likely dwarf all previous statistics. Even with such a disaster, humans may survive even if bombed back to the Stone Age.

Comets and asteroids are celestial objects that are believed to be composed primarily of space dust and frozen gases. They are born somewhere in the outer parts of the universe and are not related to the formation of our solar system. The collision between a planet and an asteroid—even one as small as a few kilometers in diameter—may release as much energy as several million nuclear weapons detonating simultaneously. The 1998 movie *Deep Impact* depicts the consequences of a comet collision, including the resulting tsunamis and the threat to life on Earth.

In *Star Trek*, Captain Kirk and his crew on the *Enterprise* are depicted as undertaking an ongoing exploration to "boldly go where no man has gone before." They are motivated not only by a search for the physical components of the universe, but also an interest in discovering other life-forms. The presumption of that television series is that other undiscovered extraterrestrial life-forms may exist. In other words, the supposition that life (as known on earth) is exclusive to earth is problematic, as is the thesis that water and other elements are necessary to support life.

Life, since emerging from the primal ooze, has assumed trillions of forms. Life-forms at the bottom of the oceans have no eyes and thrive in a highly sulfuric environment that would be lethal to humans.

The preponderant form of life on this planet, the microbe, is invisible to the naked eye. Until recently we did not even know that microbes existed. Some microbes, such as those symbiotic to the human organism, are necessary for human life to exist. Others are the pathogens that pose the greatest risk of leading humankind to extinction.

THE HISTORY OF GERM RECOGNITION

Although the invention of the optical microscope preceded him, it wasn't until 1676 that Antonie van Leeuwenhoek discovered the existence of microorganisms. Building on that discovery and the work of others, Edward Jenner, in 1796, developed an immunization process for smallpox by introducing a small amount of vaccinia (cowpox pus) into an afflicted eight-year-old boy. Although it was already known that the use of a weak form of a disease provided immunity to the virulent version, this was the first time that it was applied in human inoculations.[33]

By 1885, Louis Pasteur had revolutionized the inoculation process by developing an artificially weakened form of a pathogen microbe (an attenuated vaccine) in lieu of a naturally weak form of the actual disease organism. By injecting his new vaccine, Pasteur healed a nine-year-old boy who was stricken with rabies.

Pasteurization is another process (developed by Pasteur, for whom it was named) that treats ingestible liquids so that they don't cause diseases in animals and humans. Pasteur is credited with the statement, *In the field of observation, chance favors only the prepared mind.* It is worth noting that Pasteur took great legal risks in treating patients, because he was not a medical doctor. If the results of his work turned out unsuccessfully, he might have been tarred and feathered (figuratively speaking). In today's tightly regulated environment he could not have created all of the benefits for humankind that his work spawned.

In recounting the pioneers who recognized the role of germs in the disease process, it would be remiss to overlook a contemporary of Pasteur, the Englishman Joseph Lister. At the inception of his surgical career, hospitals practiced surgery under unsanitary conditions. Lister employed one of Pasteur's methods, known as "asepsis";

---

33 When smallpox was finally eradicated in 1979, it had already killed an estimated three- to five-hundred million people in the twentieth century alone.

that is, he exposed wounds, clothing, surgical instruments, hands of surgeons and the air in operating rooms to an antiseptic chemical known as carboxylic acid (phenol). Prior to Lister's institution of this process, patients had just as much chance of dying from postoperative infections as from their illnesses.

EVOLUTIONARY CONSIDERATIONS

The relatively slow cycle of human evolution was considered in chapter 3. We're the slowpokes! Animals and plants have been crossbred for thousands of years to produce genetically altered hybrid offspring (which are the opposite of purebreds).

In 1866, a monk named Gregor Mendel published the results of his experiments on the alteration of peas. Mendel chose pea plants for his experiments because he could observe inheritance patterns occurring in two generations within one year.

Building on the pioneering work of Mendel, geneticists now carry out their breeding experiments with species that reproduce much more frequently. Fruit flies (*Drosophila*) and bacteria are commonly used for this purpose. Fruit flies reproduce in about two weeks after birth, while bacteria, such as the *Escherichia coli* (*E. coli*) found in our digestive systems, reproduce in only three to five hours. (Note: although *E. coli* normally colonizes the lower gut, it may have pathogenic consequences if introduced elsewhere in our bodies.)

Darwin postulated that life evolves so that the fittest survive to produce new generations and, in so doing, propagate the species with the most survivable mutations. Microorganisms (bacteria and viruses) have those same survival capabilities, albeit at a much faster evolutionary rate.

When Alexander Fleming accidentally discovered penicillin in 1928, it was thought to be the ultimate solution to conquering infections (at least bacterial infections). Because of their capacities to mutate rapidly in menacing environments, microorganisms seem to have the ability to keep a step ahead of medical science in the development of therapeutic agents. In fact, entirely new strands keep popping up to compound the threat to human existence.

A short history of a few of the hundreds of pandemics in human history will demonstrate how real is the threat:

- Smallpox (165 to 180 AD) killed five thousand people per day in the Roman Empire.
- The Black Death (bubonic plague [1346–1350]; incorrectly thought to be the worst epidemic of all time) resulted in twenty-five million European deaths.
- Influenza (Spanish flu, 1918–1920) killed a minimum of an estimated seventy-five million people.
  Now, let's include more recent numbers:
- Asian flu (1957), two million dead.
- Hong Kong flu (1958), one million dead.
- AIDS (1960–present), thirty million dead.

This is a short list that doesn't include cholera, malaria (one million deaths each year), yellow fever, and all of the so-called diseases of childhood (measles, mumps, and chicken pox).

Prognosis for Humankind

Most species of life that once lived on this planet are now extinct (98 percent). Earth has witnessed many periods of extinction in its long history. In fact, there was a period sixty thousand years ago when almost all life became extinct. Based upon such history, is there any reason to believe that human life is *not* at risk of becoming extinct?

Taking that thought one step further, is it unreasonable to believe that our universe is part of a succession of one or more previous universes that failed? It is now believed that there is a universe parallel to ours.

We speak of a big bang being the genesis of our current universe while prior to the big bang all of the energy of our universe was concentrated in one source.[34] What was the origin of that energy (or infinitely compact mass)? Was there a previous universe of energy that stopped expanding (our current universe is in its expansion phase) and then coalesced back into one energy source that gave rise to our big bang?

Today, if we think of human extinction, we think of wars or comet impact. Even with weapons of mass destruction, wars are unlikely to extinguish the entire human race. Comet impact is a more likely candidate, and such a collision will surely happen sometime in the future. The greatest imminent danger to survival, however, is the biologic threat from microorganisms.

---

34 Energy and mass are the same, one being convertible to the other, as Einstein demonstrated when, in 1905, he created his formula $E = mc^2$.

Bacteria and viruses are mutating faster than medicine and drugs can keep up. The likelihood of a coming plague that will engulf the world is real.

The Federal Drug Administratin (FDA) is the governmental guardian that is assigned the task of ensuring that new drugs developed by pharmaceutical companies are relatively safe for use. All drugs have side effects that extend beyond their intended therapeutic purposes. It is the role of the FDA to ensure that those side-effect risks are within acceptable limits. Performing that role for any one drug frequently takes years and millions of dollars before approval can be given (at least in the United States).

In the face of imminent mass-infection risks, it would be prudent to take whatever measures are necessary to speed up the process including expanding the parameters of acceptable risks for new drugs. In such a risk/reward scenario a few more might be at risk but the overwhelming majority would benefit.

Finally, we put very little effort into proactively anticipating the next plague and creating ongoing research efforts to prepare for it. Perhaps money and political stumbling blocks need to be addressed (as with the Manhattan Project that created the atomic bomb). As it stands now, massive efforts come about only as reactions to new threats that surface, which is too long after the first warning signs and deaths appear. Too little, too late.

There is one final consideration that may have an impact on the survival of humanity that may come about as a result of scientific and medical advances. It now appears that physical immortality may be possible (see chapter 5). With that, concerns have surfaced about life expectancies in the near future becoming multiples of what they are today. With fewer people contributing to economic productivity, can the cost of an aging and retired society be sustained in the long run? Will the demands for marvelous new treatments and replacement organs overwhelm the ability of the political and economic systems to provide them?

The final verses of Genesis speak of the corruption of humankind. Genesis 6:5 reports that God saw that the wickedness of humankind upon the earth was great, and that all human thoughts were directed toward doing evil. God regretted having made humankind and announced, "I will blot out humankind whom I created, from off the face of the earth—from man to animal, to creeping things, and to birds of the sky; for I have reconsidered My having made them" (Gen. 6:7).

Can we overcome the failures of our history and promote lessons from our successes? A response to this dilemma will reflect one's pessimistic or optimistic outlook. Choose for yourself!

Epilogue

. . .

Commonly, the epilogue is where an author summarizes, ties together, or otherwise provides some after-thoughts on what was previously presented. I will diverge from that practice to introduce an entirely new subject that is personal to me; an account of my lifelong fascination with airplanes and my passion for flying.

From time immemorial, humankind yearned to defy gravity and soar above their evolutionary fate of being bound to the earth. The mythical father and son team of Daedalus and Icarus fulfilled that fantasy by mimicking the wings of birds as an attachment to their bodies. In the real world, Leonardo da Vinci toiled on the mystery of flight and left behind many designs of bird-like wing devices. All failed.

Flight of heavier than air bodies from a level field mandates two requisites: lift and propulsion. Birds accomplish both by the unique way that they flap their wings. It is pure muscle power that man is incapable of duplicating. Attempts to copy birds was a dead end.

It took two bicycle maker brothers from Dayton, Ohio, to solve the problem. Through years of work and experimentation, Orville and

Wilbur Wright produced a machine that incorporated lift with fixed wings (not flappable) and propulsion with an internal combustion engine of their own creation. That combination resulted in a flying machine that lifted from the sands of Kitty Hawk, North Carolina, in 1903. Surprisingly, little attention was paid to that breakthrough accomplishment for more than a decade until World War I discovered a use for aeroplanes.

War has always sought new ways to kill. Early history saw small innovations such as the cross-bow that could penetrate armor being developed from the bow and arrow. Gun powder was a sea change that led to the terror of the machine gun in World War I. During that *War to End All Wars*, the new aeroplane was used as an adjunct in support of ground armies, that is, it was used primarily for observation and, to a small extent, as aerial artillery. That all changed at the outset of World War II.

The Japanese attack on Pearl Harbor forever disabused the long standing notion that capital ships were the pride of a nation and provided security. The airplane became the new pre-eminent tactical and strategic weapon. The following quotation from chapter 4 is worth repeating here:

> *"You can't say that civilization don't advance, however, for in every war*
> *they kill you in a new way."*
>   Will Rogers (*New York Times, December 23, 1929*)

I grew up during World War II. The headlines and newsreels of the day incubated my enthrallment with airplanes. Who could not cheer the heroism of the Doolittle raid on Tokyo? Airplanes assumed life-like qualities when the Flying Tigers painted sharks on the nose of their pursuit planes. Bombers like the B-17 Flying Fortress became iconic.

My fervor for airplanes and flying has remained with me since my childhood. I will end with an ode that is at the heart of those who love flying:

High Flight

Oh! I have slipped the surly bonds of Earth
And danced the skies on laughter-silvered wings;
Sunward I've climbed, and joined the tumbling mirth
Of sun-split clouds, — and done a hundred things
You have not dreamed of — wheeled and soared and swung
High in the sunlit silence. Hov'ring there,
I've chased the shouting wind along, and flung
My eager craft through footless halls of air. . . .
Up, up the long, delirious burning blue
I've topped the wind-swept heights with easy grace
Where never lark, or ever eagle flew —
And, while with silent, lifting mind I've trod
The high untrespassed sanctity of space,
Put out my hand, and touched the face of God.
                    — *John Gillespie Magee, Jr*

Sources

• • •

I am indebted to the following for source materials.

Acton Institute
Adams, John Quincy
American Enterprise Institute
Annals of Internal Medicine
Atkins, Robert
Baker, Edward
Baudelaire, Charles
Beautiful Mind, A
Becker, Ernest
Ben-Gurion, David
ben Zakkai, Jonathan
Bershady, Harold
Bible, the
Bloodless Revolution, The
Book of Revelation (see also the Bible)
Booker, Christopher
Boston Globe, the
Brandeis, Louis
British Broadcasting Company (BBC)

Wattenberg, Ben J.
Webster, Daniel
Weimar Republic
Wells Fargo Economic Group
What's Behind the Entitlement Crisis
White, Harry Dexter
White House Committee on the Economics of Climate Change
WHO Census
Wilson, Edward O. (*Consilience*)
Woods Hole Oceanographic Institute
Wordsworth, William
Wrinkle In Time, A

About the Author

Dr. Bob, as he is known to his companions, is an alumnus of Weequahic High School in his hometown of Newark, New Jersey.

He funded his engineering degree from the New Jersey Institute of Technology by playing the saxophone at various gigs.

After graduating from NJIT, he served in the United States Air Force while continuing to play the saxophone off duty to save for a dental education after the completion of his military service.

Graduating from the University of Pennsylvania School of Dental Medicine, Dr. Bob practiced dentistry for forty-nine years, during which he married his current wife and was involved with the raising of five children (his, hers, and ours).

Aside from his other undertakings, Dr. Bob pursued a passion for flying and became an FAA-licensed commercial pilot.

Dr. Bob lives with his wife, Betty, in Florida. He continues to play the saxophone and now pursues his love of flying with radio-controlled scale airplanes.